C++

....

Programming Basics
for Absolute Beginners

1

DISCLAIMER

The information contained within this eBook is strictly for educational purposes. If you wish to apply ideas contained in this eBook, you are taking full responsibility for your actions.

The author has made every effort to ensure the accuracy of the information within this book was correct at time of publication. The author does not assume and hereby disclaims any liability to any party for any loss, damage, or disruption caused by errors or omissions, whether such errors or omissions result from accident, negligence, or any other cause.

WHY YOU NEED THIS BOOK

Your program code needs to be written as step-by-step instructions using the commands that your choice of programming language understands. It means reading your programming manual to learn which commands you need to use for what you want your program to do. In the "Hello World" example you would first need a command that prints "Hello World" onto the screen, and then you would need a second command to print it again multiple times, without writing multiple print statements.

Check out this example. To make things simple I am using old-school basic with line numbers - probably because I'm a retro-freak.

10 print "Hello World"

20 goto 10

The best structure for writing any program code is to make it clear and easy to follow. Some programmers put multiple commands on one line which can make your code difficult to follow if you are trying to iron out bugs. Spreading your code over multiple lines actually makes the program work better and becomes more readable.

Another recommended practice is to separate each part of your program code using REM Statements. REM (short for Remark) allows you to put comments before each section of code to remind you what each part does. This is especially useful if you wish to edit your code at a later date.

```
10 rem Set Up Variables

20 let A=1: let B=2

30 rem *******
```

40 rem Print Variables to Screen

50 rem *******

60 print A,B

Anything after the REM command is ignored by the computer and you can use as many REM statements as you want to make bigger gaps in your code for easy reading. Other programming languages allow you to use blank lines or indent the first line of the routine.

Now I will show you how to structure the entire program code. Remember that the computer needs to follow step-by-step instructions so you need to write each instruction in the order you want it to run.

CONSTRUCTION OF CODE

Set up screen resolution and variables: The first section of your program would set the screen resolution and the variables.

Read information into arrays: If you have information you want to put into an array using the DIM command then you can use a For/Next loop and the READ command. It is best to place the data statements for the array to read from at the end of your program.

Set up main screen: This is the section where you would use a subroutine (GOSUB Command) to set up the main screen. In a shoot-em-up type game you would have a routine that draws the sprites and game screen and then returns to the next line of the code it came from.

Main Program Loop: Once the program is up and running the main program loop jumps to various routines using subroutines and then returns to the next line in the loop.

Program Routines: It is good structure to place all the programming routines after the main loop. You would have separate routines that update the screen, check for joystick input, check for collision detection and so on. After each check you return to the main loop.

Data Statements: Finally you can list all the data statements at the end of the program which makes it easier to find and correct if need be.

Table of Contents

13

INTRODUCTION

You are probably writing more Microsoft Access programming code then you need to.

This means wasted coding time, more code maintenance and possible debugging. This article applies to all versions of Microsoft Access, not just Access 2007, but many new features of Access 2007 allow you to do zero coding to do tasks such as bulk emails, form control resizing, scheduling tasks, date picking, formatting, etc.

I have reviewed tens of thousands of lines of programmers' code, not just in Access 2007, and have found that many lines of code are being written in areas where much less code was needed to do the same job. Here's the technique that will save much time.

Did you know that your data tables in Microsoft Access 2007 can be used to control your Access 2007 program and write code for you, if they contain metadata.

Metadata is data about data. You have actually been storing and using metadata since you started using Access 2007. When you choose a color for a form textbox label, you are instructing Access 2007 to remember this color and run program code that creates that color each time that label is shown.

Ok, here is an example of how you could save yourself from writing many lines of code by using metadata that you have stored in an Access 2007 data table.

Here's an example of using metadata. You have some reports to be printed every Tuesday and some that need to be printed every Friday. You could write some Access 2007 code to print the Tuesday reports by writing:

If Weekday(Date) = 3 then 'It's Tuesday

```
DoCmd.OpenReport "Tuesday Report A"

DoCmd.OpenReport "Tuesday Report B"

DoCmd.OpenReport "Tuesday Report C"

DoCmd.OpenReport "Tuesday Report D"

DoCmd.OpenReport "Tuesday Report E"

End if
```

You would then write some more code for Friday reports:

```
If Weekday(Date) = 6 then 'It's Friday
```

```
DoCmd.OpenReport "Tuesday Report A"

DoCmd.OpenReport "Tuesday Report B"

DoCmd.OpenReport "Tuesday Report C"

DoCmd.OpenReport "Tuesday Report D"

DoCmd.OpenReport "Tuesday Report E"

End if
```

Now let's write these 14 lines of code with one line 7 lines of code.

```
Dim rs As DAO.Recordset
```

```
Set rs = CurrentDb.OpenRecordset("Table
Name Containing Metadata")


Do Until rs.EOF


If ![DayOfWeek] = Weekday(Date) Then


DoCmd.OpenReport ![ReportName]


End If


rs.MoveNext


Loop
```

These 7 lines of code would not need to be changed or added to even if the 10 reports increase to 50 reports in Access 2007 or any other version of Access.

The Access 2007 data table would only need to store the report name and the day of week, just two fields of data. This means easy maintenance and no future code changes.

This technique can be used for running a set of queries with a specified sequence. Use metadata when linking to external data sources by including paths, file or table names, and specifications. You can automate importing or exporting data by storing import and export specifications, formats, and storage paths.

CHAPTER 1

ADVANCED TIPS TO HELP PHP PROGRAMMERS IMPROVE THEIR PROGRAM CODE

Ever since it made humble beginnings around two decades ago, PHP programming has witnessed a rapid climb, going on to become the most popular programming language for all Web applications. Numerous websites are powered by PHP programming code while an overwhelming majority of Web projects and scripts rely on this popular language for their development.

Owing to the huge popularity of this development language, it is seemingly impossible any PHP programmer to say that he lacks even the basic working knowledge of PHP. In this tutorial we aim to help those at the learning stage of this programming language, willing to roll up their sleeves and let their hands get dirty with this language. These simple programming tips will aid in speeding up the proficiency of the development process while making the code cleaner, responsive and offering optimum levels of performance.

Implement a cheat sheet for SQL Injection: SQL Injection can prove to be a really nasty thing. This is a security exploit wherein a hacker can dive into your database by making the most of a vulnerability in the programming code. MySQL database is commonly implemented in PHP programming code so being aware of the things that you should avoid can prove to be really handy if you are planning to write a secure code.

Be able to differentiate between your comparison operators: An integral part of

PHP programming is comparison operators. However, some programmers are not as adept at sorting out the difference between them as they ought to be. In fact, many documentations lay claim to the fact that most programmers are incapable of telling the difference between the comparison operators at first glance! Failure to identify the difference between "==" and "===" is a big blot on the reputation of any programmer.

Favour the use of str_replace() over preg_replace() and ereg_replace(): As far as the overall efficiency is concerned, str_replace() proves to be much more efficient as opposed to some of the regular string replace expressions. In fact, statistics show that str_replace() improves the efficiency of code by as much as 61% compared to some of the regular expressions such as preg_replace() and ereg_replace(). However, if your program code comprises of nothing but regular expressions, then preg_replace() and ereg_replace() will prove to be much faster and efficient that the str_replace() function.

The use of ternary operators: Rather than use an if/else statement altogether in your PHP programming code, consider the use of a ternary operator. They are effective in terms of freeing up a lot of line space for better readability of your programs. The code looks less clustered and it is easier to scan it in the future for any unexpected errors. However, be careful that you do not have more than one ternary operator in a single statement. Very often, PHP gets confused regarding its course of action in such situations.

Use a PHP Framework: Use of a PHP Framework is seemingly impossible for every project that you create. However, the use of such frameworks as CodeIgniter, Symfony, Zend and CakePHP helps in greatly reducing the time required for developing a website. A Web framework is typically a software that bundles itself along with functionalities that are commonly needed, aiding to speed up the development process. By letting a framework handle all of the repetitive tasks required for website programming, you can work on the development process at a much faster rate. Less coding you have to take care of, lesser will be the testing and debugging requirements thus letting you speed up with the overall process.

Make correct use of the suppression operator: The @ symbol is typically the error suppression operator. Place it in front of a PHP expression and it will simply instruct all errors in that particular statement to show themselves. This is a very handy variable if you have doubts over a value but would not want them to show up when the script is run. Many PHP programmers, though, very often use this error suppression operator in an incorrect manner. The @ operator is unusually slow and can be rather costly if you are planning to write a code keeping its reultant performance in mind.

While alternate methods exist to sidestep the errors brought about by the use of the @ operator they may result in accidental side-effects and should only be used in areas from where they cannot further affect other areas of the code.

Rather than use strlen, opt for isset: If you are planning to implement a function that checks the length of a string, opt for the use of isset rather than strlen. Isset allows your function call to work as much as five times faster than the other functions. Also note that by the use of isset you can have a valid function call even if there is a non-existent variable.

While this is a small change to make, it nevertheless adds up to a leaner and quicker code, akin to all of the aforementioned tips that we have presented in this chapter.

PHP Programmers is a business solution service provider company specializing in website development, PHP framework programming and CMS development. Contact us to hire our team of expert and dedicated professionals who will serve your business as per your requirements.

THE IMPORTANCE OF USING COMMENTS IN PHP PROGRAMMING

PHP is a very versatile language, allowing for programmers to make applications according to their various tastes or styles. But one thing all programmers should maintain is the ability to comment effectively. In essence, commenting can save hours of time perusing code months down the road- and is often required by employers.

Comments aren't parsed by the PHP engine, so they are only visible to those who are viewing the original source code of the file. This is great for documenting what each code block does, all while keeping the casual visitor to a website oblivious to the extra comments present on the application they are using.

Unlike HTML comments, PHP comments aren't even visible in the source code of a website. HTML comments are visible to the general public, which can potentially lead to the stealing of code or may even help hackers exploit applications. PHP comments aren't output to the browser at all, so they are completely safe from prying eyes.

There are actually three operators that we may use to tell the PHP engine that we want to use a comment. Single inline comments can be used with the "//" and "#" operators. For multiple-line comments, we use "/*" and "*/" respectively to indicate what is a comment and what is actually PHP code. While the first two operators are synonymous, the last one discussed is the only one that can perform multiple line comments with relatively little work.

Unknown to most, PHP comments can also be used for more practical scenarios, such as troubleshooting. Expert programmers will find they have a problem with their application, and comment out different blocks of code to see what is causing the error. While it is usually in new code blocks, this method will indeed show that sometimes the problem is due to program code interacting wrong, which can in effect mean the problem is anywhere in the application.

Commenting in PHP is also great to use in selection structures, since PHP has long been known as a hard to scale language. Once files start getting big, it can be dizzying to try and remember which loops and selection structures go where, and what they do. By commenting out every closing bracket, and what it is in relation to, the problem is easily fixed. This is often mandatory for programmers who work for employers.

CHAPTER 2

LEARNING JAVA PROGRAMMING CODING LANGUAGE

There are many programming languages available and each of them is suitable for another program or application. There are people who have learnt only a few programming languages and who use these because that is what they know, bust most of the times software programmers will use the programming language that is required by the application they are creating. Java is one of the most frequently used programming language and writing in this language is somehow different from the usual Pascal or any C/C++ version but that does not mean that learning the java code is harder than learning Pascal or C++. Nowadays there are numerous applications written in Java and its terminology it may seem a bit harder in the beginning but anyone can write in this programming language, that's for sure.

When looking into a new programming language, most people would like to know if it is easy to learn and work in. If you compare it to C or C++, you may discover that indeed, using it can be more straight forward. This is due to the fact that Java has far fewer surprises compared to C versions. C and C++ make use of a lot of peculiarities so learning and mastering them all can be a daunting task (for example, temporary variables hang around long after the function that created them has terminated). Being more straight forward, Java is a bit easier to learn and to work with. Java eliminates explicit pointer dereferences and memory allocation/reclamation, for example, two of the most complicated sources of bugs for C and C++ programmers. Out of range subscripts are easy to find, as Java is able to do add array bounds checking. Others may argue that it seems easier to work with because there are very few examples of extremely complicated projects done using it, but the general accepted idea is that it is somehow easier to master than C or C++.

Learning Java programming is not very difficult, especially if you are familiar with other, more basic, programming languages and you know for sure what you want to create using it and it has a series of benefits compared to C and C++. First of all, code written in this programming language is portable. Code written in C and C++ is not and this makes Java more practical (for example, in C and C++, each implementation decides the precision and storage requirements for basic data types.

CHAPTER 3

TIPS FOR LEARNING A NEW PROGRAMMING CODE

Learning a new programming language, if you already know how to program in a comprehensive language like C, C++, Java etc, is not difficult. That's because the concepts and principles of pretty much all languages are the same, they are used to instruct the computer to do meaningful things to the programmer. Computer (programming) languages are pretty much like human languages but they are a little bit more explicit. In order for the computer to do something, you should instruct them in detailed instructions. Before trying to lean a new programming language you should consider the 3 following things:

1) Is the language you are going to learn interpreted or compiled? Interpreted languages execute code by first reading one instruction, compiling it and then executing it. On the other side, compiled languages first compile the whole source code into binary code that is readable by the processor and then execute it step by step. Most of the programming languages fall into the compiled category. Knowing whether the language you are going to learn is complied

or interpreted will have an impact on the development process.

2) The context the language is used in. There are programming languages for any kind of work. If you are going to program things related to statistics then you are most likely going to use R, if you are going to program for Windows then the most popular language is C#, for networking the language of choice would be C or Java. You should know in advance what you will use the language for. I have seen many students trying to just learn a new language without knowing what the language is used for.

3) The IDE (Integrated Development Environment) for the language. The times when you sat and opened the notepad to program are gone. There much more powerful environments to program than just notepad. I think the IDE has a great impact on the final product you are going to produce. Good IDEs provide color-coding,

automatic filling and much much more controls. You should consult professional developers about a great IDE.

The last thing I would want you to know about is that programming is a lucrative job. It takes a lot of effort, experience, and time to become an experienced and professional developer. Some people say that you should have been exposed to programming since you were a "baby" but this is not true. Take the time to learn and practise, practise, practise.

PROGRAMMING, CODING AND WEB DEVELOPMENT LAPTOP SPECIFICATIONS

If you need to get a new laptop for programming or coding purposes and are uncertain where to start, this short guide will help you find the perfect setup for your needs.

For web developers, there are really two main paths they need to go through. If you're doing front-end web development, then you'll need a basic machine that can run a text editor and a browser to check your progress. For back-end developers things get a bit more complicated. You will need a laptop that can handle multiple tasks simultaneously like running a browser, a local server and the code editor. These might not seem like a lot, but they do require a lot of system resources so make sure you pick a laptop that's up to the task.

For game, 3D or mobile app development you'll need a high performance laptop that can render everything in real-time. Think about getting a gaming laptop if you'll be doing this type of work. Mobile app developers will often need to run a simulation of their app running in the mobile operating system, which can take a lot of system resources.

Let's have a look at some of the specs recommended for each of these types of development work.

Processor

The processor is the heart of your computer and by the number of cores and threads it boasts, it determines how many processes you can run well in parallel.

For front-end development work, you should be able to get away with a laptop that uses either a Core i3 or Core i5 dual-core processor. Back-end and mobile app developers should aim at least for a Core i5 quad-core processor, Core i7 being the best choice.

RAM

RAM or system memory helps the CPU process everything smoothly. The more your laptop carries, the better. Front-end work implies about 4-8GB of system memory installed, since you'll probably use a code-editor like Sublime Text and one or more browsers to check up on your work.

Mobile, game and back-end developers should opt for something with a bit more kick. The minimum amount of RAM should be in the 12-16GB range. This is to make sure that all your applications run smoothly together.

Hard Drive or SSD?

Every laptop needs to store and retrieve information. This is done by the storage device installed. Here you have two choices: either get a laptop with a regular HDD, that will typically cost a lot less, or get a laptop that comes with an SSD. An SSD is the newer type of storage option that doesn't

39

rely on spinning disks to store information and can be about 10-12 times faster than a regular hard disk drive.

For front-end development work, a regular HDD should be enough, but you can always look for hybrid drives which incorporate a bit of SSD technology into a regular HDD. These are a bit faster than regular hard drives and don't cost quite as much when compared to SSDs.

For any type of programming that's above front-end development, it's recommended that you get a laptop that carries an SSD. This will speed up boot times and everything you run on your computer.

Operating system

This is yet another thing you will have to think about. While Windows is perhaps the most popular operating system today, it's not quite the best choice when all development fields are concerned.

For web development you should try coding in a Linux-based OS, like Ubuntu. Mac OS also works with Windows being the last on this list. This is because you need to install different third-party software like XAMPP on Windows if you're going to do back-end work. You will have to install some of these as well on Ubuntu, but the process is much more streamlined.

Screen

The laptop screen is another factor that's important to take into account. With so many resolutions available today, it's hard to pick a laptop that's just right for programming.

Front-end developers will need a laptop that carries a screen with a higher than average resolution, since they'll need to test if their websites are responsive on a lot of resolutions. For back-end developers, this is less important. But what's true for both of these categories is the need for a secondary monitor. This can speed up development time quite a lot, since you don't constantly need to switch between applications when coding and checking the output.

Battery Life

While most developers sit at their desk when coding with the computer plugged-in, should you feel the need to code on the go, then make sure you get a laptop that's got a great battery life.

Macs are typically great at battery life, with their Air series going up to even 12 hours of battery life on a single charge.

The thing is, the more powerful hardware a laptop carries, the more battery life will be sacrificed. This is because powerful hardware eats up a lot of electricity. Most computers nowadays have devised ways of counter-acting this by dimming the display, throttling down the processor when the computer isn't used and so forth.

If you're sure you need a laptop with a great battery life, that's also powerful but don't want to pay through the nose for a MacBook, then you should invest in a secondary battery that you can take with you when you're on the move.

In conclusion, if you've run through all these aspects, you should have a pretty clear picture in your head of what your next laptop should be like.

HOW TO FIND A WEB SITE CODER

So now you know what to look for in a coder--but a much greater problem for many people is the problem of where to find the perfect coder for your project. It isn't simply a matter of posting an advertisement in a local classified section and waiting for responses--that might get you some potential candidates, but it removes one of your best tools for assessing the suitability of a coder: the portfolio.

One useful method is to post your project on freelancing programming sites, one of the most prominent of which is rentacoder.com. Rentacoder.com allows software buyers--such as yourself--to post details of your project on their directory of projects, along with some idea as to the rate you're willing to offer. Coders can then bid on your project, giving you portfolio examples, any certifications they may have, and their ideal rate for the work. Once you've checked out what they can do, you can approve their bid, place your payment in escrow, and just wait for the coding work to be done. As soon as the coder sends you the work (and as soon as you approve it), the money is released to the coder, and you can both go on your ways--your coder with his cash and experience, and you with your functioning direct response website.

There are a number of advantages to this method. Most importantly, there's the wide talent pool from which to choose--just as putting your business on the Internet gives your product a much wider potential audience than you could achieve through traditional channels, looking for contract employees (like coders) over the Internet gives you a much wider selection and a much greater chance of finding someone with the perfect skills for your job. Additionally, services like rentacoder.com greatly simplify the process of interviewing potential coders and determining prices:

most of the things that you need to know about a coder (namely, their skills and their price) is available at the rental site, just waiting for you to sort through the options and make your decision.

But it's important to keep in mind some of the disadvantages to services like rentacoder.com as well. For one, it's very difficult to get a good sense about a potential coder's personality from their rentacoder.com profile or even their skills set. Again, this isn't a problem for short-term work, but as we've discussed, the ideal relationship with a coder is a long-term relationship. Not only does rentacoder.com make it more difficult to create such a relationship by masking coder personalities, but it also makes it more complicated to hire a coder on an ongoing basis. Rentacoder.com only allows you to bid on a coder for a single project--e.g. a single website--with no simple provision for providing ongoing work.

Fortunately, these obstacles aren't insurmountable--it just requires more work on your part in order to build and nurture a relationship with your coder. Rentacoder.com automatically releases personal details like phone number and email address for all projects above $500, allowing you to contact your coder directly-- once the project is in motion, unfortunately. Before the hiring process--or if your design work costs less than $500, which it shouldn't (see below)--you can post messages to your coder on the rentacoder.com message boards or chat rooms, which is the ideal way to contact them--and there's nothing that says you can't ask for a phone number or email address in such communications to help you make the informed decision before renting a coder.

Are there other options? Of course--there's always classified advertising (on or offline), there are personal references from other business contacts, there's the possibility of emailing the designers of high-profile sites that you've seen and liked, and there's the ubiquitous Craigslist posting. But as long as you're willing to put in the effort to build a personal relationship with your coder (and to assess their personality and skills before hiring), sites like rentacoder.com simply offer too much variety and too much talent to ignore altogether.

IMPORTANCE OF CODING STANDARDS

Programming Help for Beginners

We write programs to instruct computers. When programming using a high level programming language like C++ or Java, we are using a syntax that is somewhat closer to human languages. However, we use these programs as inputs to either compilers or interpreters to be converted to computer understandable binary format. For this reason, as far as the program code adheres to the syntax of the used programming languages, the compilers and interpreters never bother about the layout or visual formatting of the program code. However, as human programmers, we ourselves need to bother about the aesthetics of the program code.

What is a Coding Standard?

A coding standard is a set of guidelines, rules and regulations on how to write code. Usually a coding standard includes guide lines on how to name variables, how to indent the code, how to place parenthesis and keywords etc. The idea is to be consistent in programming so that, in case of multiple people working on the same code, it becomes easier for one to understand what others have done. Even for individual programmers, and especially for beginners, it becomes very important to adhere to a standard when writing the code. The idea is, when we look at our own code after some time, if we have followed a coding standard, it takes less time to understand or remember what we meant when we wrote some piece of code.

Coding Standards Make a Difference

Look at the following example:

```
int volume(int i, int j, int k) {

int vol;

vol = i * j * k;

return vol;

}
```

Looking at this code at a glance, it takes some time for one to understand that this function calculates the volume. However if we adhere to a naming convention for variables and method names, we could make the code more readable.

Here are few sample conventions:

use meaningful variable names

use verbs in method names

use nouns for variables

use 4 spaces to indent

```
int calculateVolume(int height, int width, int length) {


int volume = 0;


volume = height * width * length;
```

```
return volume;



}
```

It takes more time to type this code,
however this saves far more time. This code
is far more readable than its original version.
With a little bit of effort, we could make the
code much more understandable.

The Benefits

It is not only the readability that we get
through a coding standard in programming.
Writing more secure code could also be
encouraged through a coding convention. As
an example, in C++ we could say that each
pointer variable must be initialized to
NULL.

```
char* myName = NULL;
```

This ensures that we would not corrupt memory while using this pointer variable.

Code readability is just one of the aspects of maintainability. Coding standards help a great deal with program maintainability, our ability to change programs with ease. Consistency imposed through a coding standard is a key factor to achieve success in maintaining prorams.

WHY HAVE CODING STANDARDS? A MANAGEMENT OVERVIEW

All too frequently a programmer is left to produce code, without standards or quality assurance. It is only after a major problem that the months and in some cases, the years of programming are found to be worthless. Some control on the code being produced is essential - and this starts with a well documented Coding Standard.

No matter how busy you are, a Coding Standard will be a time saver in the long run - it is fundamental to good programming. Coding Standards and programming productivity go hand-in-hand. Adhering to a Coding Standard will lead to a significant increase in development productivity, whatever the programming language. A consistently applied set of Coding conventions will standardise the structure and coding style of an application, so a programmer can readily read and understand other programmers' code, as well as their own code.

Good Coding Standards result in precise, readable, and unambiguous source code that is consistent and as intuitive as is possible. The object of a Coding Standard is to make the program easy to read and understand without cramping the programmer's natural creativity with excessive constraints and arbitrary restrictions.

Maintenance Costs

Following a Coding Standard will increase productivity, not only to system development, but increase productivity in enhancing and maintaining systems as well. And it is also important to control maintenance costs- these can constitute most of the lifetime cost of software.

To reduce the high maintenance cost, it is essential to have code written that can be easily deciphered and enhanced by any other programmer in your Company. This is important, as usually very little software is maintained by the original programmer.

Enforcing the Standard

All the programmers should agree on the Coding Standard. Once agreement has been reached, the Standard must be enforced, as part of quality assurance. The use of the agreed coding techniques and good programming practices play an important role in software quality and performance. By consistently applying a well-defined Coding Standard, a team of programmers working on a software project is more likely to yield quality software system code that is intelligible, error free, cost effective and maintainable.

Here then are some ideas to help create your Coding Standard. Make it short and to the point:

Readable Code

The code must be created so that it is easy for other programmers to understand. It should not be written only with just the computer in mind. The code should be easily readable, with lots of white space.

Blocks of Code

Blocks of Code should be broken into sections that are well defined and understandable procedure chunks. It may be helpful to use a "Main Line" to split a lengthy procedure.

Code Indentation

Those "If" "If" "Else" "Else" constructs are hard to follow, if the indentation of control structures is inconsistent.

Variable Names

The variable naming convention should be well thought out, meaningful and consistently applied. The variable name should describe the content of the variable. Try not to have abbreviations, unless they are consistently applied. The standards for capitals, Camel or Pascal case need to be set.

Procedure Names

Much as for variable naming conventions, procedure names should describe their purpose.

Code Documentation

No matter how well the code is written, changes or enhancements will eventually be required. Time should be spent when actually writing the code, commenting on the intent and technical aspects of the code. This will save time and effort later on.

In addition to external documentation, all code should be liberally documented with comments. Each procedure should have a heading with comments describing the input, output and function of the procedure.

Complex Constructs

There is always the temptation to use the latest and greatest feature - this is true especially with inexperienced programmers. Complexity and the esoteric will make a program code difficult to follow, maintain and debug. Simplicity, above all, must be enforced.

Keep the Coding Simple

If another programmer cannot understand, at a glance, what the Code is all about, then the Code is badly written. So often it becomes necessary when debugging or enhancing code, that the code be rewritten. This is a costly exercise for the company as well as being a non-productive and wasted effort.

Isolate Complex Code

There will be the occasion when simplicity must give way to complexity, when functionality or performance is required. In these cases (hopefully, few and far between), the complex code should be isolated in a "black box" library procedure.

Reusable Code

The Coding Standard should include the gathering and documentation of reusable Code. With reusable Code, that is Code that is not duplicated throughout an entire organisation, the programmers will build programs faster - and programs that run faster. Using less Code means greater productivity and faster development cycles. By using the same Code repeatedly by every programmer in every project, errors are identified and eliminated sooner.

HOW TO GET CHEAT CODES

Cheating may spoil the game experience for some players, but for impatient gamers who want to unlock all the game's secrets, cheat codes are a blessing in disguise.

Why Cheat?

Cheat codes are a sequence of passwords, keystrokes, or other tools used to unlock features and bonuses, or to aid the player to finish the game. Cheat codes are sometimes used by game programmers to debug or analyze flaws in the game; sometimes, the cheat codes remain with the game code when the game is released. Some video game publishers and developers may purposefully put cheat codes into the game to satisfy gamers.

Common Kinds of Cheat Codes

For a password to be properly called a "cheat code," it must directly affect the gameplay. Visual effects and new sound effects from a secret password are not considered cheat codes. Here are some of the most common cheat codes in video games.

* God mode grants a player temporary or permanent invulnerability.

* Unlimited resources may add more credits or mana to a player's resource pool or mana meter. Some cheat codes may do away with caps, and just give you unlimited resources to work with.

* No clip is a cheat code used in action games and shooter games, and gives you the

ability to walk through walls and other obstacles. No clip cheats may also give you the ability to fly.

* Unlocked levels may include secret levels or rooms that can only be accessed with a cheat code.

* Unlocked abilities and weapons, including infinite ammunition and new spells, can be attained through cheat codes.

The Internet

The Internet is your best resource for cheats. There are very few games without a cheat code, and there is no computer game out there that is completely cheat-proof. Here are some of the cheat codes and cheating tools you can get from the Internet:

* Actual codes. You can simply type the name of the game in a search engine, add

"cheats" to the search string, and you can find an assortment of cheat codes on the Internet. Remember to surf safely, because many cheats may contain spyware or malware.

* Strategy guides and walkthroughs are text documents that contain the complete details on how to play and complete a game. It may be a full plot for a role-playing game, strategies for a first-person shooter, or the complete movelist for a fighting game.

* Saved games are usually used for console and PC games, where everything has been unlocked. Saved characters for role-playing games may also be used to give you a head-start in a game, although cheated and hacked characters can easily be detected in multiplayer games.

* Trainers are used for many games where the manufacturer did not leave or release a cheat code. A trainer is a program that runs in the background of the game, and exploits loopholes in the programming code to allow a cheat. The cheat is activated through a

series of hotkeys, usually bound to any of the function keys (F1 to F12).

* Cheat hardware. When games still ran on cartridges, the Game Genie was a popular piece of hardware used to input cheat codes. Similar cheat hardware also include Pro Action Replay and Game Shark.

Programming

For those who want a challenge, programming is a very good way to cheat. Even the most thoroughly tested games in the world will have a few loopholes here and there that programmers and modders (people who modify games) can use to explore cheats and the limits of the game. Programming a cheat may be seen as unethical by some people, but some game programmers use the valuable information provided by people to make a more enjoyable, stable, and less vulnerable game.

CHAPTER 4

THE A+ PROGRAMMING LANGUAGE

The programming world, is very vast, and you have to do a lot of research, in order for you to be able to grasp, any programming language in its entirety.

You will also find out very early, in your journey to becoming a great programmer, that there are many programming languages out here, which are necessary for you to learn; if of course you would like to be a great programmer and create that great application that you've always wanted to create.

In this chapter, we are going to talk about the A+ programming language and all its important features.

A+ is said to be a descended of the A programming language, so if you know about the A programming language, you will have some type of idea of what A+ programming language, is really all about.

I don't want us to get confused here, so I should mention that A+ is also a name used for an IT certification, which many individuals who would like to become a computer technician, pursue to further their careers.

The knowledge of the A+ certification, will definitely help you with your job, if you are a computer technician.

When you decide to obtain an A+ certification, you will be able to troubleshoot, maintain, customize, repair, install and help people with their computers.

You are going to be an awesome person, to many people when you are able to utilize your knowledge, to help them solve their computer problems, so that they are able to use their computers, to do their job.

However, in order for you to be able to get there, you do have to have, some type of valuable knowledge on your own about computers; in order for you to bring some real, sound contribution to someone's life, by fixing their computer.

When you obtain an A+ certification, it will help you to be a valuable person to someone fast, you will also be on your way to be an awesome person to other people for real.

Anyhow we are here to speak about the programming side of A+ and that is what we are going to do.

First of all, A+ as we mentioned before is a descendent of the "A" programming language, it was created by Arthur Whitney in 1988 at Morgan Stanley.

The purpose of A+ was to provide its users, applications that are considered to be useful in the business world, because these same applications are developed in computational-intensive business environment.

In 1992 an A+ development group was formally created to upgrade and maintain this programming language.

The plus in the A+ programming language name, is referring to the electric graphical user interface, which means that you won't have to just use a command prompt or a terminal, because there is a GUI that you can use to accomplish, the development your business applications, with A+ programming language.

A+ offers advantages, of an interpreter in a fast-paced development arena, it also offers an admirable floating point performance, which helped this programming language become the language of choice when it came down to fixed income applications for the business industry.

A+ is a programming language that is for actual programmers, and for those programmers who are dedicated, to creating software and website applications.

If you are the kind of programmer, that code just for fun, then you should definitely get you a copy of the A+ programming language, so that you can easily start to program.

You can easily obtain a copy of the A+ programming language, if you do a simple online search, you won't have to pay for it either, because it is freely available under the GNU General Public License.

If you are a beginner and are now just starting to learn A+, don't hesitate to do your research, to gain more knowledge and information, so that you are able to program, with this great programming language, because A+ is for those who are just beginners as well.

A+ has many useful features, such as dynamic loading of user, compiled subroutines, and a modern graphical user interface with many widgets.

The A+ programming language also has an automatic synchronization of widgets and variables, and finally but not least, it also has an asynchronous execution of functions associated with variable and events.

A+ also offers extensions, which are used for graphical user interface and inter-process communications, as well as a module for storing and loading objects such as functions, variables and dependencies.

A+ also offers an extension for built-in database systems, so that you are able to manage your databases, using the A+ programming language.

You can also implement a spreadsheet in A+, if you would like to accomplish things with a spreadsheet within your application development.

A+ has a good graphical display capability; therefore, you would be able to visualize your data on that spreadsheet using A+ without any major problems.

If you do encounter some problems, visualizing your graphical data on A+, then know and understand, that your knowledge about A+ is limited, and you need to do more research in order to be able to completely master the A+ programming language, and have the ability to properly use the graphical display capability of A+.

The language also includes a special font to properly display special characters, and it uses a healthy subset of hieroglyphs, which you can also find in APL.

A Programming Language (APL) is one of the first programming languages, which was created with the invention of the computer.

APL was created for mathematics, with an emphasis on array processing.

We will talk more about the APL programming language on other article posts, for right now let's focus on A+.

It would be helpful to mention though, that APL inspired the creation of A+, because A+ is an array programming language as well, which was created more than 20 years ago, with the help of APL and the A programming language.

The need of real-life financial computations are met with A+, which is used to develop applications, which are used in computationally-intensive business environment.

A+ is only found in UNIX operating system, because the interpreter-based execution environment of A+ is implemented in C.

Although, the core A+ interpreter, which does not include a GUI or an IPC, have been ported to Microsoft Windows.

A+ is truly a powerful and unique language, because it draw, most of its features from APL and A programming language.

The same primitives with a very similar syntax are used in A+; but the security found in A+, is much better and a good implementation of A+, is more efficient, than any APL system that is currently online.

One of the advantages, which you would find in A+, is that you can find some extensions, such as a graphical user interface

76

and inter-process communication, as well as a modules for storing and loading objects (functions, variables, and dependencies), and even a built-in database system, within the A+ system.

This means that you can define auxiliary functions, inside a module, which would not be accessible to the outside world, to develop your application with the A+ programming language.

Variables, can also be defined within modules, which would allow the module to track the internal state of the module.

A more secure style of programming is achieved, through these features; which essentially allow users to write, good structured programs.

If you are the type of programmer, who does not have a style of programming just yet, you will find your style with A+, once you start to use this programming language.

Self-discipline is a key feature in writing good code as well, you have to be able to follow directions and pay attention to details.

When you don't follow directions and pay attention to details, then any bug may enter your code, and it could take you forever to find out where the bug is within your code.

Finding a bug within your code, could take hours or even days, in the worst case scenario, making your life a living hell.

The A+ programming language is an array programming language at a high-level model, which gives programmers access to entire sets of data, so that they are able to easily manipulate their data.

As a programmer, you don't have to resort to loops to manipulate individual data found on an array.

A+ is an array oriented programming language, which puts data together; unlike object oriented programming language, which uses loops to decompose data, to its constituent parts.

Needless to say, through programming, you will find a great way to learn new things in computing, and learn about the technology that we use every day.

However, you do need to continue to upgrade your skills, so that you are able to become, who you want to be in the programming arena.

Anyways, back to the fact of the matter, A+.

In A+ the individual elements of an array argument, can be applied independently to a primitive scalar, which is one of the primitive functions of A+.

A primitive scalar can be applied to an entire array, so that it provides a syntactically efficient and implicit control structure.

Ordinary arithmetic functions, certain mathematical function, and logical tactics as well as comparison functions, are all part of the scalar primitives in A+.

Let me say that again in case you missed it, mathematical functions, logical functions, comparison functions and ordinary arithmetic functions are some of the scalar primitives found in A+.

Each individual element of an array in A+, can be affected by the scalar primitives, which is the main purpose of scalar primitive.

Also, scalar primitive can not only manipulate each element of an array in A+; but it can also have full control of an entire array.

Developers who are using A+ can use this feature to control an array very efficiently and write a very sophisticated programming code.

I hope you know of each of the functions we just mentioned and what do they do or how they function.

But, if you don't let's talk about them a bit here at King Info Life, and you let us know what you think.

Mathematical functions are similar to a machine that has an input and an output.

Mathematical functions are not bound to a set of numbers only, mathematical functions can be used for all sets of numbers, such as complex numbers, decimals, real numbers and even other functions.

Unlike mathematical functions, which can be used for any set of numbers, arithmetic functions are only found to be utilized with whole numbers only.

I hope you are able to make the connection between mathematics and computers, because mathematics, is one of the reasons why we are able to create our technology today.

Logical functions are your conditional statements you will often see in programming; such conditional statements is: if (this) {then... that} else {do... nothing}, it has to make sense, because it is using logic.

If the condition doesn't make any sense, then your code will not work properly, and you may spend hours trying to fix it.

So make sure that your conditions make sense, before you use them within your code, to save you a headache.

Comparison functions, are used to compare arrays, within the A+ programming language, as well as each member of the array.

The comparison functions test elements of an array, to analyze if they are equal to each other, or not equal to each other; also to analyze if one array element is greater than the other array element and to figure out, if an element is between two elements of an array.

Alright, now let's talk about another type of primitive function called structural functions; which is used in A+ programming language, mainly to rearrange the indices of its arguments.

In this case it receives an argument or any kind of an array, which can be rearranged, however the user may want the elements of an array to be rearranged.

For example if you would like to shuffle an array, then you would use a structural function to accomplish this task.

Another type of primitive function is the specialized function, which is used by a developer, to be able to sort arrays and invert matrices.

In other words, the array would be changed completely, giving your new array a whole new structure, because it is a different array.

In order to have very good abilities in understanding how to study any subject, you have to have a clear head.

You need to let the spirit of The Most High power guide you through this deceptive world.

He will come for you and you have to be ready to receive Him in glory, but you need to let Him guide you so that you are not under the trap of the snake.

The snake is real and if you fall for all of its deceptions, you will surely be gone, and won't be able to learn more about A+.

CHAPTER 5

WHY DEVELOP A MICROSOFT ACCESS PROGRAM?

Although Microsoft software makes it easy for a beginner to develop applications, there are times when you need to go beyond the basics. MS Access will allow you to create some fairly nice applications using the wizards and also the design tools. If you are looking for even better functionality and to have more control over your application then it may be time to develop a Microsoft Access Program.

MS Access has always had a built in macro language. Macros are a great tool in that they are a halfway house between general system building and programming. There is a macro for practically anything you want to do in MS Access. You could for example create a macro to delete a record and then display a message saying it has been deleted. It is advisable to experiment with the in built macros before looking at programming.

Prior to MS Access 2007, one of the main drawbacks of using macros was that they offered no error checking. Without this there is no way to know what caused the system to crash. A macro will throw up a general fail message, but this is not always useful. Program code will pinpoint the error or give you a much better idea as to what has gone wrong. You could then write more code to get around or trap for this error.

Microsoft Office uses a common programming language called VBA or Visual Basic for Applications. There are some differences between say Excel VBA and Access VBA. In fact PowerPoint and Outlook also have their own version of the language. However, despite the differences, if you can write code in one Microsoft program you will pretty much be able to find your way around another.

Try creating a macro to do a specific task and then try and write program code to do the same thing. This will start you off slowly and get you used to developing code. As you gain more confidence you will find certain code can be used again and again. It is also a good idea to create a code bank - a database of your favourite code routines that you can use again and again. This will save you time as you can just pull up the code routine and won't have to worry about how to write it again.

To begin writing a Microsoft Access Program you can either learn from a book, the internet or go on a course. It takes time to become a good developer, although VBA is one of the easier languages to learn.

Let's recap what we've learned in this chapter:

Experiment with macros before moving to program code

VBA is the program language used in Microsoft Office

Create a code bank to hold your popular code routines

CHAPTER 6

CODE REVIEW - UNDERSTANDING STATISTIC CODE ANALYSIS

The Static code analysis is one study of software that is carried out without performing programs that are built through that particular software. In some cases the study is carried out on some versions of source code, in others some object code. This term is mostly used in relation to the study performed by automated tools, with man-made research known as program comprehension or program understanding.

The complexity of the research made by tools, differs from those considering behavior of a persons statements made with those which include the full code of the program analysis. Using information achieved from the research varies from highlighting the expected coding errors to a formal method which have arithmetically proved the properties regarding any program.

There is a dispute that reverse engineering or software metrics are the methods of static analysis. An increasing commercial usage of static research is in the confirmation of software which is used in the critical systems when identifying the expected vulnerable code. Formal method is a term that is useful in the research of software as well as the hardware whose outcomes are attained through use of precise mathematical ways. The mathematical methods used includes axiomatic semantics, operational semantics, denotational semantics, and abstract interpretation.

Some techniques of such analysis are:

Model checking - mainly reflects on the system that has a limited state or may reduce to limited state by idea

Data-flow analysis - This is a network-based method used to gather information regarding possible set values;

Abstract interpretation forms the outcome that all the statement has the state of a theoretical machine. This over estimates the behaviour of the said system, this is therefore made easier to come up with the result without the expense of incompleteness. Though abstract interpretation is sound.

Using assertions in programming codes was initially suggested by logic. It is a tool for some but not all programming languages

It is proven, excluding the theory in the state of programs, that it is limited and in small amount when trying to locate all possible run-time errors, generally any kind of abuse of the specification on the final judgment of the program, is not decidable as there is no mechanical method used to answer truthfully in regards to the program that may or may not display the run time errors. As per the undecidable questions, one can try to give an approximate answer.

CUSTOM CODING BASICS AND MORE

Internet has changed the way we read, perceive and understand the world through our computer screens. Even if you are not directly affected by something like custom coding, you should be conversant about it. It is better to know about coding for website design layout, search options for beginning an online business or to get accustomed with how things work for the more curious intellectuals.

Custom coding is an object oriented PHP coding of high quality. The fusion of supporting tools and product can provide an efficient Content Management System (CMS) platform or custom code for the website.

Writing a customized code for your website can be easy. Code based on the minimum requirements is much prompt when compared to a customized CMS. Added functionality to the website with help of this customized coding is a bonus. Modification of a well written and documented code can be changed easily. The programmed code has the most important features of speed and functionality.

The coding, based on changing technology can be changed quickly. Clear know-how of your website program is possible with custom code only. Different section or pages of website can be given diverse styles with the custom programming method. Accommodating coding format can provide the required layout and even the appearance of the website. Before you start the project, scribbling down points for customized coding proves to be a better option.

What is your requirement-who will write the code?

Use of the code for website and hosting conditions.

Features you need for an efficient site.

Number of users coming to the website.

Site maintenance and updating

The applications like Customer Relationship Manager (CRM), data mining and Enterprise Resource Planning (ERP) were more rigid and costly in last decades. As the speed of internet has improved, the users expect quick business online.

Web programming has improved considerably and affordable web development is available to everyone interested in e-commerce. Bill Schrader quoted "almost overnight the internet's gone from a technical wonder to a business must".

Many companies offer to do the daunting task of coding for your website at nominal rates. You need to plan out your requirements and the desired strategy and tools for best PHP application development. Make sure you research properly and then give your project to a company for PHP coding. The web world is very vast to accommodate all businesses and hence we need to capture the attention of our clients for better trade prospects.

CHAPTER 7

BEST PLACE TO LEARN PROGRAMMING

Nowadays, Programming is not just for computer geeks anymore, it has become a "must have skill" to stay in the market.

Coding is an incredibly much valuable skill for employers and members of any business team. With programming, you can make your own website, mobile app. If you learn to program, you can take your entrepreneurship skills to the next level.

Everyone holds the equal potential, and the chance to learn programming language easily. Today, we will show you a list of top websites that will help to learn to program.

Code Academy

Code Academy is one of the best places to learn programming languages. It is a well known first stop for those who are looking to begin their programming education.

Students can learn to code from their several different courses like:

- HTML & CSS
- JAVA
- PHP
- JavaScript
- Make a Website
- Ruby on Rails
- Angular JS
- SQl
- Python
- jQuery
- MIT Open Courseware

If you want to learn to code in a high-class university level - then MIT Open Courseware is the best place for you. So take advantage of this opportunity and check out top courses like:

Introduction to Computer Science and Programming, Introduction to Programming in Java and Practical Programming in C.

Coursera

Coursera is an educational technology company that has offered more than 2,000 courses from 150 top institutions around the world.

If you want to improve the beauty of your CV, you can get a paid certificate from coursera. So learn to code from Coursera and become a top programmer.

edX

edX is the leading online-learning platform that is the open source instead of for-profit. Founded by the top universities like Harvard University and MIT in 2012. you should know that you'll learn about the latest cutting-edge technologies and theories.

edX offers tons of free programs, including courses on programming.

Khan Academy

Khan Academy is actually my favorite to place to learn programming. If you are looking to learn to program in an interactive way then khan academy is the best place to do so. Offering free programs like:

- ✓ HTML / CSS
- ✓ JavaScript
- ✓ SQL

✓ Animation

and many more...

Udacity

Udacity is the project of Stanford University. It is one of many sites that make college courses available online for free. Stop thinking that how to learn programming.

Learn high-quality courses from the high quality website.

Udemy

Founded in 2010, Udemy is an online learning platform through which you can not only learn to program every programming language. But you can also learn almost every skill available on the internet. Yes!

you heard it Right. There are many courses you have to pay for, also, there are several free programming courses, which are taught via interactive video lessons.

Google Android Course

Want to learn Android development, why not learn from the king of the internet Google. Offers free courses on mobile/android development (beginner to expert level). Android development is the trending skill that you can learn to get a well-paid job.

CHAPTER 8

WHAT CODING LANGUAGES ARE USED TO DEVELOP IPHONE APPS?

While it may sound like a very technical undertaking, anyone with a good knowledge of object oriented computer programming can easily develop iPhone apps. However, due to restrictions placed by Apple, not all object oriented programming languages are suitable for would be developers. Here is a detailed guide on what programming language is best and how best to approach the task.

Apple restricts all apps meant for launching on its Apple stores to be based on Objective C as a programming code. Objective C is a hybridized form of the more universal C programming code. It is possible to create passable applications using other languages and then using a wrapper API to make it look like Objective C but this may not always work.

In order to develop a good app that will get enough popularity with iPhone users, you need to use a Mac computer. For the best results, go for one with an Intel based processor, preferably running MAC OS X. As such, you will not have to trouble yourself with thoughts about compatibility of the applications you develop as they will already be optimized for use on iOS devices.

The next step is actually easy. After setting up your MAC, go and download the iPhone app developer SDK (Software Development Kit) from the Apple website. Apple provides the SDK free of charge and it contains everything you need to begin including the environment XCode as well as the simulator that allows you to test the apps before launching them.

Brush up on your OOP (Object Oriented Programming) skills especially as they apply to Objective C. It has in many ways similarities with Java as it hides the complexity of the underlying hardware leaving you to concentrate on the technical aspects of the application itself and not the platform on which it will run. Today there are plenty of free online tutorials to guide you.

Start by writing simple programs. Being too ambitious to begin with can cause you numerous problems in the future. It is best to play it safe by beginning with a set of manageable projects and gradually qualifying to more complex and challenging tasks as your skills and confidence increases. Unlike more safe OOP languages like Java, a single misplaced byte in an Objective C code may lead to your program crashing as a whole.

After testing your application sufficiently on the simulator, you need to migrate to the real iOS environment. To do this, you need to register first with the official iPhone developer program. You will need to pay a joining fee of $99. After you have signed the agreement to abide by Apple's code of conduct, return the form to begin testing your application on a real iPhone environment.

Becoming a good Apple devices application developer is more about having the right skills and tools rather than being a professional programmer. Learning the right object oriented coding will help you to develop iPhone apps that are ready to launch on the actual devices. Once you get registered as a developer, you can launch them online and await them to be downloaded by enthusiasts.

VISUAL BASIC 6: INTELLECTUAL PROPERTY AND CODE OWNERSHIP

Visual Basic 6 is still used in a huge array of applications today. In particular, a large number of administration systems were written with a combination of a VB6 Front-

End and a Microsoft Access or SQL Server database Back-End.

Using Visual Basic 6 as the Front-End was a good idea at the time. But Visual Basic 6, released in 1988, cannot be purchased and extended support stopped in 2008. The number of willing programmers with the necessary skills and software resources to maintain an obsolete VB6 is rapidly diminishing. And the rates charged can be high.

Any company still using a VB6 Front-End system is in danger of an unsupportable system falling apart at the seams. Making "just a simple change" to the system becomes a major operation - and expensive, if at all possible to do.

Supporting antiquated software is a "no win" situation. And changes are always needed - with new security restrictions, with the advent of newer operating systems, with new administrative functionality being required.

Code Ownership and Copyright

The question of code ownership and copyright is being asked with increasing frequency. The problem of Code ownership of the VB6 Front-End can be a real threat - where a company is highly dependent on its administration system.

The usual rule "if you pay for it, you own it" does not apply with program code - ownership and copyright usually reside with the author of the software.

Obtaining the Code

There is need for total control by a company of the development process. But the code might simply not be available - the original programmer may have moved on to better and greener pastures. Frequently, obtaining the code leaves a company open to extortion.

But just possessing the VB6 code will not solve the ongoing development problem.

Even if the Visual Basic 6 code is available - will it run? Usually a large number of third-party OCXs (Custom controls) and DLLs (Dynamic-link libraries) have been incorporated. And the installation software and licenses for these add-ins are hard to come by. Most of the VB6 third-party software companies are now defunct, or have been taken over by other companies.

And, due to the primitive nature of VB6, the Front-End system will have incorporated many OCXs, DLLS and APIs (application programming interfaces) - for system information, reporting, data grids, resizing, calendar controls, buttons, tooltips, dropdowns, etc, etc.

Then, in trying to set up the programming environment, difficulties may include conflicts between DLL and OCX versions and registration problems - commonly known as "DLL hell".

Code Ownership must be determined from the outset

This may seem like 20/20 hindsight, but for future reference:

When a developer is hired to create an administrative system, the company's ownership of the code should be agreed from the start.

To enforce this, after each new release of the software, the code should be deposited onto a PC within the company. And to make assurance doubly sure - it must be demonstrated that the code compiles, and that it can be deployed to all the users.

Neville Silverman, based in Sydney Australia, has been a Visual Basic programmer and Microsoft Access programmer and Database design specialist for many years.

He has created numerous Microsoft Access databases, SQL Server Databases and Microsoft Visual Basic systems for clients. He develops and supports software systems for the small to medium sized business. Administrative systems are custom built to fit company requirements - software solutions that are cost effective, efficient and user-friendly.

Optimising Access Database systems is his speciality. He has extended the useful life of many an Access Database system, avoiding the effort and cost of an SQL Server upgrade.

COMPUTER PROGRAMMING BASICS - LANGUAGE YOU CAN USE IN CREATING PROGRAMS

Individuals who want to learn computer programming and the languages that can be used in making programs must first be familiar with the basics. Languages employed in programming should be one of your primary considerations. Prior to creating programs, it is crucial that you know the different types and levels of programming languages. Among these are:

1. Machine Level Language

We all know that computers work in bits and bytes and it reads and understands binary digits 0 and 1. While you are free to make a program in any language you want, it has to be transformed into the languages of 0s and 1s before it can be implemented.

It means you need to write a program or to convert your written program into machine language. And this is no easy task. It is nearly impossible to memorize a long sequence of 0s and 1s for each instruction you wish to be executed.

Yes it is true that before the development of high level languages, the ones used in making programming codes are machine level languages. These days, however, this level of language is not used anymore in designing computer programs.

2. Assembly Level Language

This level of programming is only one level higher than low level or machine languages. This is actually the reason why creating a program using such languages isn't a piece of cake, although, the programming code produced is pretty understandable.

Until now, there are lots of programs for embedded technology that are created in assembly language. The program that's responsible in transforming assembly level programs into machine level programs is called the assembler.

3. High Level Language

These computer languages are easier for humans to understand. It entails clear statements for making each instruction. Languages that fall in this category have different purposes. There are languages designed for web programming; some for desktop applications, while others can perform both tasks.

One thing to bear in mind though, high level language isn't easy for the computer to understand. This is where the importance of an interpreter or a compiler comes in. Such programs transform the programming code into a language form the machine can understand.

Aside from these three basic levels of languages, another generation of programming language is now being designed. This is dubbed as the fourth generation language which is designed for those who have very minimal or no programming experience.

Developers of such language want these inexperienced programmers to learn to prepare their own code. This is also the very reason why high level languages like Java already came with these systems. These enable a person to write a programming code without memorizing every function.

Bear in mind that no matter what programming language you want to learn, you need to have proper understanding of the basics. If you're not familiar with programming language basics, you will not be able to make a program in that specific language. It is advisable that you take up computer courses so you'll be able to learn more than just the basics of computer programming.

CHAPTER 9

THE ADVANTAGES OF THE OPEN SOURCE WEB DEVELOPMENT PROGRAMS

Open source web development programs have been around since the beginning of the birth of internet. It is a development system that allows effective and complete accessibility to a program's source code. These programs are created by the people, maintained and used by them too. Open source software is different from the program developed by certain companies as it is exceptionally affordable. Here are some of the advantages related to the use of these development programs.

The technology is great to improve your web site and make it even more effective. Not only this, you can do almost anything that you can imagine on your computer using these approach. There are many big web development companies out there that support open source web development programs wholeheartedly as the system is one of the most safest and honest mode of development. Since it is extremely accessible, other developers are able to analyze it for any flaws or viruses.

The cost of this technology is very reasonable. The web sites for open source technology can just operate without having to spend a dime for license and server fees. The audit ability of these programs is also high since it is easily accessible contrary to the closed source system that makes its customers trust them without question.

Flexibility that comes with this methodology is extremely high. The owner of the product or program code is not obligated to be in connection with a certain organization or person. The code is able to be accessed by anybody and thus can be customized according to the individual's preferences.

The ownership of the system is not fixed. The users of this technology are allowed to own the code of the products or programs created with no hassle with encryption issues. Unlike closed source programs that have encrypted codes, users of the open source technology are free to view the code and make adjustments needed to remove flaws and other problems.

META-LANGUAGES AND THEIR USEFULNESS FOR USER DRIVEN PROGRAMMING

Meta-languages describe the structure of information to enable this information to be searched more easily by software systems. XML (eXtensible Markup Language) has emerged as the most important of these Meta-languages and is the base for many languages. XML standards are important for the Semantic Web, many computer based reasoning systems, and for communication between different software applications. Alternative representations of information should not be used in any system being developed now unless the author has examined XML based standards and found them insufficient. Such a situation is highly unlikely. Any software system that does not use these standards will have difficulty communicating with other software systems. Use of a generic standard keeps open the possibility of communication with the widest possible range of other software systems. Use of a domain specific standard targets the communication to a particular domain.

Extensible Markup Language XML is an important standard in the development of ontologies. This language allows for the construction of text documents in which the relationship between concepts is represented. Because it is an accepted standard it is possible to use XML on any type of computer. Further developments such as Resource Description Framework

RDF add a layer of standardisation of semantics, above the standardised syntax of XML. It is also possible to represent diagrammatic, and graphical information using a variety of XML called Scalable Vector Graphics (SVG).

These open standard languages can be used for developing the program code of models. It is proposed that software and information represented by the software, be separated but represented in the same open standard searchable way. Software and the information it manipulates are just information that has different uses, there is no reason why software must be represented differently represented differently from other information. So XML can be used both as the information input and output by the application, and for the definition of the model itself. The model can read or write information it represents, and the information can read from or write to the model. This recursion makes 'meta-programming' possible. Meta programming is writing of programs by other programs.

The purpose of this is to provide a cascading series of layers that translate a relatively easy to use visual representation of a problem to be modelled, into code that can be run by present day compilers and interpreters. This is to make it easier for computer literate non-programmers to specify instructions to a computer, without learning and writing code in computer languages. To achieve this, any layer of software or information must be able to read the code or the information represented in any other. Code and information are only separated out as a matter of design choice to aid human comprehension, they can be represented in the same way using the same kinds of open standard languages.

CHAPTER 10

JAVA APPLICATION PROGRAMMING - COMPONENTS AND VARIOUS DEVELOPMENT TOOLS

Java is a very popular programming language which involves various syn-taxes from C++ and C language. But it has a simpler model then these two other complex programming languages. It has object model and low-level facilities for the users which makes it easier and simpler to use and understand.

Java Application Programming was developed by a person named James Gosling in 1995, at a present date subsidiary of Oracle Corporations, which was then called as sun Micro-systems. JVM or Java Virtual

Machines are needed to run these java applications which are compiled to class file format. Irrespective of the computer architecture JVM is always required to run this type of files. Java Application Programming is specifically designed to have the least amount of implementation bottlenecks. It works on the principle of "write once, run anywhere" pattern.

It means once your write the coding of the program, you can use it on other destination too. You don't need to write it again and gain every time. Java is not only a programming language but also a software platform, which lets the application developers to use this simpler, class based and object-oriented programming language instead of the complicated high level languages like C and C++.

But the major disadvantage of using Java Application Programming is that, the programs written in Java are slower and need more memory space to get stored then the programs written in C language.

For that concern, the sun Micro-systems have been working upon java technologies under the specifications of the Java community process. And have achieved remarkable success in the context of introducing Just in time compilation model to run these applications in the year 1997-98. Some new language features have been added to the language like inner classes, optional assertions and String-buffer class etc.

Java has compilers in it, which conduct the basic functions whenever an application developer writes a code with syn-taxes and characters to run a particular Java Application Programming code.

For faster speed a company names Systronix has developed a micro-controller called jStik based on a line of java processors. A standard edition for Java Application Programming language has various components. It uses multi-tier architecture for database connectivity. It uses XMl files to store data and writing codes. JDOM is used for outputting XML data from Java code.

All the components of java work together to perform a given task, and such components are listed below:

1. Development tools and APIs as Java complier, Java debugger, Javadoc and JPDA

2. Deployment technologies could have sub-parts like Java web-start and Java plug-in

3. User interface tool kits are swing, AWT, sound, input methods, java 2D and accessibility.

4. Integration APIs are RMI, JDBC, JNDI, and CORBA.

5. Core APIs are like XML, logging, beans, Locale support, Preferences, Collections, JNI, Security, Lang, Util, New I/O and Networking

6. Java virtual machines are of three types as, Java hotspot client compiler, Java hotspot server complier ad Java hotspot VM runtime.

The various Java platforms are:

• Solaris

• Linux

• Windows

• And others.

CHAPTER 11

HOW TO WRITE YOUR
VERY FIRST PHP PROGRAM

Advanced programmers know a secret. The secret that they know relates to how a PHP program is constructed.

Here is the secret:

"Complex programs are built up from simple programs. If you can learn how to create a simple program, you can learn how to build a complex program, no matter how complicated."

A program can be constructed of only a few lines. They always start the same way. Start with the PHP start tag, followed by your programming code, and last by the PHP end tag.

Example 1:

Line 1: <php

Line 2: // your program goes here

Line 3:?>

The PHP program shown above has only 3 lines. Line 1 & 3 are the start and end tags, line 2 is your functional code. In this case however, line 2 is a comment and will not perform any specific action other than to remind you of something. Comments are not processed by the interpreter. Once a comment is encountered, it is basically ignored.

Example 2:

Line 1: <php

Line 2: // this is one comment

Line 3: // this is another comment

Line 4: // this is the last comment

Line 5:?>

The code in example 1 behaves exactly as the code in example 2. Even though example 2 has 2 more lines. If you noticed, the additional lines in example 2 are only comments. Once again they are ignored by the PHP interpreter (PHP Engine).

If there is one comment or multiple comments, the interpreter will act the same way. It will ignore any comments that it finds.

Example 3:

Line 1: <php

Line 2: // below this line is a real PHP programming command

Line 3: echo 'My First Real Program';

Line 4:?>

In example 3 you will see your first functioning PHP program. The 'echo' command was added to this program, located on line 3. An 'echo' statement is a built in PHP command that will output whatever follows it to the screen. Anytime you want to output something using PHP to the screen, web browser, or visual display. Use the simple 'echo' command.

As you can see, the words 'My First Real Program' follows the 'echo' command. It is very important to enclose the words that you want 'echoed' on the screen inside single or double quotes. This way the echo command knows from what character to start with, and

what character to end with, as it generates the output to the screen.

When the echo command is called, it takes the contents inside the quotes, and sends it out to the screen - minus the quotes. So the output would be:

My First Real Program

Example 4:

Line 1: <php

Line 2: // the next line is the first echo command

Line 3: echo 'You are ';

Line 4: // the next line is the second echo command

Line 5: echo 'learning how to ';

Line 6: // the next line is the last echo command

Line 7: echo 'program in PHP.';

Line 8:?>

The output to this program would be:

You are learning how to program in PHP.

When you start programming, there is no limit to how many comments and commands you can enter in your program. Go ahead, try it yourself. As you get better you won't need so many comments to remind you of what you are doing in your program.

Complex programs are made up of simple programs. Learning how to mix simple commands together, along with PHP start and end tags makes a fully functioning PHP program. As you are learning, a good suggestion is to add as many comments as you need to help remember what you are doing. Comments are like taking notes that you can refer back to. As you get better at programming, you will naturally enter less comments. The PHP 'echo' command outputs characters to the screen. Enclose all characters after an 'echo' command with single or double quotes.

CHAPTER 12

DRAG AND DROP
PROGRAMMING

This chapter examines how drag and drop programming and other forms of interactive software development can assist end-users to program via the web. AJAX (Asynchronous JavaScript And XML) software is used to provide a Web 2.0 style interactive interface. This can be linked to applications and to Semantic Web information.

Lieberman [1] blames end user programming difficulties on hard to understand programming languages and techniques and argues for visualisation and translation to code to enable end-user programming. To make end-user programming easier it is possible to develop high level visualised templates and translate these into program code. The Dagstuhl report [2] argues that existing programming languages are not sufficiently dependable for end-users to reliably use. De Souza [3] argues that the goal of human-computer interaction (HCI) will evolve from making systems easy to use to making systems that are easy to develop. A template system will assist in this. Ko [4] explains that end-user programmers must be allowed to focus on their goals, and an important part of the solution is to visualise the whole program execution not just the output, so it is necessary to show the user the whole program flow not just text based bug reports. A simple illustration of the techniques that can be used to further this research area is a demonstrator for meta-programming of XML (eXtensible Markup Language) based drag and drop trees [5], this example was created with AJAX (Asynchronous JavaScript And XML), a Java applet or Python were other options investigated.

The code acts as a translator between the XML representation of the trees and interactive graphical representations. This allows open standards platform independent end-user programming. The example is based on the Scand dhtmlxTree [6] and this makes it possible to enable many other programming actions such as adding and deleting nodes, and to create other controls. Repenning [7] argues that visual programming languages using drag and drop mechanisms as a programming approach make it virtually impossible to create syntactic errors, allowing for concentration on the semantics", and Rosson [8] also advocates this technique. Such techniques could be used with other Semantic Web-based information representations implemented with languages and structures such as XML, RDF (Resource Description Framework), and OWL (Web Ontology Language), and provision of other controls. These controls could then be used as graphical components of a simulation system made available over the web. As well as being used for web-based visual programming an environment such as this could also be employed as an interface to PC based software, or as a translator between systems. Semantic languages provide a higher level declarative view of the problem to be modelled. Coutaz [9] explains that "An interactive system is a graph of models related by mappings and transformations." This would fit in well with the structure of RDF, which is also a graph structure.

It is important to investigate new ways of enabling collaboration between all those involved in software creation and use. The use of Semantic Web languages for declarative programming can ease the translation between different representations of information, and ease interoperability between systems. This translation or 'Program Transformation' allows for writing in one representation or language, and translating to another. This is particularly useful for language independent programming, or for high level and end-user translation to a language more easily interpreted by computer systems. The solution to many interoperability and software problems involves programming with Semantic Web languages rather than just using them for information representation. This will make translation for interoperability easier and more reliable, and further improve the maintainability of software systems.

The research will involve using and building a visualised Semantic programming layer on languages such as AspectXML, XForms, SPARQL, and XQuery all explained in [10] and Meta languages [11][12] to create software and to build an environment for high level end-user programming. This programming environment can be used for creating programs and an environment for end-user programming. The environment can be computer language and system independent as one representation can be translated into many computer languages or Meta languages. Tools such as Amaya [13] can be used for creating and editing Semantic Web applications and documents. This research is a test case for an approach of collaborative end-user programming by domain experts. The end-user programmers can use a visual interface where the visualisation of the software exactly matches the structure of the software itself, making translation between user and computer, and vice versa, much more practical.

To enable generic end-user programming functionality it is important to develop 'information representation languages' based on Semantic Web declarative programming languages. Standardisation in XML/RDF enables use of declarative rules for web services. This environment also has to provide a visual development interface for end-users in a similar way to that of Unified Modeling Language (UML) for professional developers. Repenning [7] and Engels [14] argue this.

JAVA PROGRAMMING, A HELLO WORLD PROGRAM

Java is the new trend amongst the world of programming languages, The most famous languages were C and C++. The C/C++

languages depended mainly on pointers and memory allocation techniques to actually utilize memory space to store data.

In Java there are no referencing, Pointing and memory allocation required, instead we use objects.Objects are children of the class or function you declare,

This makes Java easier to use, and it is a lesser stress for the processor.

For your ease, IDEs are very helpful in running huge lines of codes,

so if you are interested in Java then the recommended IDEs are

Eclipse and Netbeans.

Here is a sample Hello World program code in JAVA

The IDE, I used here is Eclipse Galileo

Import Java.Util.*;

public class HelloWorld

{

public static void main (Strings[ ] args)

{

System.out.println ("nHello Worldn");

143

```
        }


        }
```

Output

Hello World

So this shows us, hopefully that Java is a much easier language to use and compose rather than C or C++. The reason being that java is not just a language that simplifies the processing speed, but it also has an excellent format to show where you are at the moment.

for example

The proper way to write a Function in JAVA is

YourFunction   yourobject   =   new
YoourName();

This means that yourobject is the object of the function YourFunction()

So now you can reference any data through YourFunction using the dot " . " operator.

this makes writing codes easier and the execution speed or time complexity is reduced as well. so if you are looking for a language platform to take up, then JAVA might be the best one for you.

CODE GENERATORS FOR RAPID WEB DEVELOPMENT

As a web developer, one thing that helps me to rapidly develop web applications is to use a common application framework that is flexible and robust. Additionally, I like to use code generators to build code for custom applications I build for my client. My most powerful code generators, create code for interacting with the local database dedicated to my website.

Normally, it is bad practice to repeat code when doing development. However, there are certain instances when this can be beneficial and assist in creating dynamic web applications. Here, we will discuss some of the many applications that I have found useful and how you can apply them to your own business.

Object-Oriented Classes

One way I enforce code reuse is by using object-oriented design. For my data access layer I create an abstract class which contains the common functionality. Next, I create derived classes which implement the specific methods which are needed for the entity model (usually a database table).

These derived classes have different fields which represent the fields defined for the table. They also contain mappings for the primary keys, any related fields that are retrieved from related tables, and custom methods for querying the database. The idea is that all of the database calls are encapsulated in the data access layer classes.

These derived classes have enough similarities between one another that it made sense for us to build a code generator to create these files from the database schema.

How to Generate Code in Your Intranet

On our intranet, we have the code generated connected directly to our database management scripts. When an administrator is viewing a table schema, they have a button on the bottom of the screen to generate the code for our data access layer. When the user presses this button, the code is immediately generated and the user can click anywhere on the code to select the code block and copy it to the clipboard.

The process of generating code is surprisingly simple. We simply retrieve the schema from the database and from that we define all the macros that are needed to substitute into a code template. These macros include things such as the script name, database table name, primary key fields, public fields, private fields, and a generated class name.

The code is output to the screen as pre-formatted text. Below this is a web form where the user may tweak any of the macro values that were generated. After making changes to these values, they can click a submit button which regenerates the code using the custom macro values. Of course this step is optional. The user may simply choose to copy all of the program code and paste it in their code editor and continue making changes that way.

Table Administration

In my website administration panel, I have a lot of pages that are built for managing database tables. I have a very capable library which handles all of the heavy lifting for paging through a table of records, creating a new record, editing and deleting a record. This is an object-oriented class that takes a variable number of parameters.

To create a new administration area, I just need to instantiate this class, define all of the required properties, and then call a method called "Process". The resulting file is usually no longer than 25 lines of code. Creating these files doesn't take very long when done by hand. However, I knew that creating a code generator for these server-side scripts would save us a lot of time.

Again, the key to accomplishing this goal was to first read the database schema for a table to get all of the field definitions. From these definitions, it would be a simple matter to create the code from an existing script template. I just define macros for all of the properties I need to substitute in the template. As the table schema is read, I build these properties which are later substituted in to the template.

Special Considerations

When generating code, it is important to keep in mind how the script is going to be used. In my data access layer scripts, I know that they are usually two directories beneath the website root. Because of this, I know that any relative links need to go up two levels to get to the site root.

Another important area to consider is form validation. There are certain constraints you can place on a web form to limit the amount of characters a user enters into a text field. You can even make Boolean fields display as radio buttons labeled "Yes" and "No". Date fields can display using a specialized date picker.

Other special data fields can be displayed based on the field name. For example, fields containing the word "Password" can be displayed as password fields. I use fields with the name "created" and "modified" to track when a record has been changed. Fields that have the text "email" could be validated to make sure they contain a valid email address. Also, fields that have the text "postalcode" could be tested for valid postal codes.

I try to build my code generator so it is as smart as can be. The thinking behind this is that the developer can easily remove extra code that was added if they find too much validation is being done or the wrong type is done. The more work you can save for the developer, the better off you will be in the long run.

CHAPTER 13

AVOID THE CYBER THREAT BY USING A SAFE PROGRAMMING LANGUAGE

The Problem

Since the existence of networked, automated information systems, the so-called "Cyber-Threat" has been known to be a major security and business continuity risk. One of the very first worms, the "Morris-Worm", destroyed the e-mail infrastructure of the early internet. The Cyber Threat is not thoroughly understood even by many executives of the software industry, and the situation amongst the software user community is even worse. An Asian nation-state actor recently subverted the Google Mail login system by exploiting a weakness in internet explorer used by Google employees. The same Asian nation state is also suspected to have illegally downloaded the full design blueprints of the largest European jet engine manufacturer.

The Cyber Threat is real and may have grave long-term consequences for those at the "receiving end" of a cyber attack.

The Solution

Unfortunately there is no "silver bullet" solution to this problem. Rather, a holistic solution comprising technology, business processes, user education and security rule enforcement must be employed to properly secure valuable data. The determined support of the CEO, CIO and CFO is clearly required to achieve that. CFOs understand that there exist strategic business risks, which are very difficult to be quantified in monetary terms, but they know that these risks might kill the whole business if left un-addressed. For example, criminal accounting practices of mid-level managers could kill any company, so the CFO will have to ensure the books are regularly audited by an independent authority. The same amount of diligence will be required to secure the confidential data of companies against the Cyber Threat.

This chapter is about a key aspect of defending against the Cyber Threat - securing software. It is important to note that, again, there is no "silver bullet" to secure a critical software system, but many of today's security flaws (such as "Buffer Overflow Exploits") could be avoided simply by using a Safe Programming Language. This kind of programming languages will make sure that low-level Cyber Attacks are automatically thwarted by the system infrastructure.

What is a "Safe Programming Language"?

As with many subjects in information technology, there is no authoritative definition of the term. Salesmen and consultants bend the term to suit their needs. My definition is simple: A Safe Programming Language (SPL) assures that the program runtime (such as the heap, stack or pointers or machine code) cannot be subverted because of a programming error. An SPL will make sure that a process will immediately terminate upon detecting such a low-level error condition. The Cyber Attacker will not be able to subvert the program runtime and "inject" his own, malicious program code. The programmer can then inspect the "remains" of the terminated process (such as a core file) in a useful manner to analyze and rectify the programming error.

Examples of Safe Programming Languages (in alphabetical order): C#, Cyclone, Java, Sappeur, SPARK Ada, Modula-3, Visual Basic.Net

Examples of Unsafe Programming Languages (in alphabetical order): Ada, Assembly Language, C, C++, Fortran, Modula-2, (Object-)Pascal

What should I do as a Programmer?

Whenever you start a new software development project, select a Safe Programming Language, instead of chosing the "industry standard" of unsafe languages like C or C++. There exist high-performance languages like Cyclone, Modula-3 and Sappeur, which can compete with C/C++ in terms of memory and processing time requirements. Don't think that you are "one of the few programmers who can write bug-free code".

CHAPTER 14

LEADING-EDGE COMPUTER PROGRAMMING STRATEGIES - MOCKING YOUR OBJECTS

One matter that I have reviewed before was unit tests. Implementing unit tests is actually something I did roughly four years in to my professional career as a computer programmer. This unique relatively easy act produced a remarkable shift on the code that I was creating. Solid calculations such as "the amount of bugs in the code" had confirmed that the concept of unit tests had done the duty of fabricating superior program code. Now to expound on the subject of unit tests, today I must talk about mocking.

What on earth is Mocking?

The term mocking is used to specify the process of limiting the coupling between your Objects (particularly at the time of unit testing). This concept allows us to take every one of the collaborating Objects and mold them (quite simply) in to shell-like constructs designed to take away coupling. For instance, let us say we have a UserService object which allows us to save and delete users. We should test out our save and delete procedures and be sure they are always doing what we expect them to be doing... but in order to test the UserService object, we'll need to instantiate and initialize a UserDao object (since this DAO object would be conducting the save/delete operations).

This causes a hassle because at this point we're not really "unit" testing, we're widening the range of our unit test to include 2 objects. This invalidates the whole purpose of a unit test, so we must do something about this travesty!

Hello Mocking.

You can 'mock' the DAO object that will allow your UserService object to interact with an empty shell of the DAO. The UserService will still be capable of calling all of the functions, and you can even get fancy and supply your choice of return values from those called procedures. This permits you to correctly map out the exact use-cases you intend to test within the UserService object.

The only caveat here is that when you mock an Object it's not as straight-forward as one might initially think. Some complications arise when your Objects define private methods or have static/final methods. In order to deal with these types of situations, you'll need to use more than just a basic mocking framework... never fear, I shall outline what I use in a second!

So, all in all, you'll have the ability to accurately test ONE single unit of your computer code and you will still be able to execute all your tests with impressive speed. The mocking frameworks Personally i have tried recently that I would suggest highly include:

- Mockito

- Powermock

CHAPTER 15

WHY IS IT IMPORTANT FOR A WEB DESIGNER TO KNOW HOW TO CODE?

Contrary to the popular belief that web designers should not worry about web development, geeky programming codes can actually help the creative bunch to a great extent. Almost every web designer has a basic knowledge about HTML and CSS. However, they often feel that a detailed knowledge about coding will make them abandon their Mac Pros, afternoon coffees and Photoshop brushes.

I do not feel that a designer's creativity can get hampered if he becomes a code jockey. In fact, there are chances that his designing skills will get better and sharper. Are you wondering how this is possible? Here are some reasons why it is important for a web designer to know how to code:

#1. Better Design

Web designers have a great knowledge when it comes to color theory and typography. However, he should always look for ways to expand his skill-set. He must make sure he becomes unparalleled with his vision and talent. Just as a painter needs to learn about bristle qualities, paint compositions and canvas types to become a complete artist, a web designer will find it easy to execute his ideas if he knows the intricate details of the development process.

#2. Better Communication

It is natural for a web designer to find the techno-jargon of the developers totally alien to his ears. And it is obvious that he will find it hard to understand when exposed to a discussion among developers. However, efforts to know coding and working with codes will make him familiar with the terms, and as a result, "meaningful" conversions with developers will help him design more efficiently.

#3. Better Expression

The official website of WordPress has a message at the bottom: "Code is Poetry". What is the meaning of this message? It means that the power to transform a code into something visual is the highest form of art. If a web designer can write his own codes, it will help him express in a better way. He will have the power to enhance his designs by creating pathways and developing wire-frames all by himself. The more he will know about the medium he works in, the better he will work in that medium.

#4. Better SEO

Why should we rule out SEO from the discussion? After all, SEO is also a part of a website. SEO helps a website get better visibility on the search engines. When a web designer is able to write codes, he is also able to design in such a way that will benefit an SEO campaign. And when a designer is SEO-friendly, it will just become another feather on his hat.

#5. Better Accessibility

When SEO knowledge meets the power to code, it creates better accessibility. A great accessibility helps in reaching more people via a website. Designers will not only develop codes for accessibility, but also understand every consideration. It will become easier for him to present information in a clean and coherent way, and visitors will find it easier to navigate.

CHAPTER 16

WHAT CAUSES RUNTIME ERROR IN COMPUTER PROGRAMS?

Sometimes you are browsing some pages of a website and the program just pop out a message stating there is a runtime error. It slows down what you are searching or looking at. It could also be agitating to see these happening. However it is good that you learn about the causes of it and understand why some programs simply have it.

Runtime error often appears in a message box, stating some form of computer programming code or codes together with the definition on what is wrong. It is usually happens during the execution of certain programs. Depending on the error, the program or browser may close and blocked. One cause of this could be the occurrence of conflicts with the TSR, Terminate and Stay Resident Program in the computer and the applications. This could be easily resolve by using the Task Manager and choose to 'end task'. Other than that, some software simply has errors. The developer or programmer may have not anticipated such error and had come out with software that leads to these issues. It could be solve by installing patches which the developers build to improve the programs. Yet another cause is the memory problems. This has to do with the motherboard and hardware of your computer. Best ways to counter this problem is to ask a technician's help as you might not possess the right skills to deal with these things. Computer virus could also contribute to this problem. It will harm the programs and other computer applications and affect the speed of execution or process. It will be helpful to often download and update your security software in order for it to be ready to protect your computer from dangerous virus which will leads to error in various forms.

When you encounter another round of runtime error, you can identify the cause and ways to handle it.

CHAPTER 17

MICROSOFT ACCESS PROGRAMS

Microsoft Access has undergone many changes over the years, but still remains the world's most popular PC desktop database. Whether you need a simple database to log names and addresses or a full blown invoicing system, Microsoft Access can handle it reasonably well.

When looking for good Microsoft Access programs there are a few things to consider. First and foremost you will want something that not only solves your business problem, but is also robust and does not fall apart. A good MS Access program will empower the user. By this I mean it will allow the user to create their own questions, otherwise known as queries, to interrogate the database. It is not much good to anyone if the software is locked down and you have to constantly pay for amendments and updates. The software should be unlocked and give you the ability to make any changes you need.

Some Access database systems can be created with little or no programming code. In fact, the less code the better. One of the great things about the programs in the MS Office suite is that they can all communicate with each other. Why not have an Access program that can talk to Excel? You may wish to output your database invoicing statistics into MS Excel for accounting purposes. Perhaps make MS Outlook automatically email your monthly sales report.

Software should be sold at a reasonable price and should only do what you asked for. Too much software these days is overblown with unnecessary features that you may never use. Make sure any Microsoft Access programs come with a decent illustrated user guide. You don't want to have to second guess what the application does. Also make sure you can demo the software first to determine if it is going to fit your needs.

CHAPTER 18

MEET THE MOST USED SOFTWARE PROGRAM ON YOUR COMPUTER

When buying a new computer, people consider lots of variables like screen size, memory, processor speed, price and more. However, when it comes to choosing a web browser, most people have little idea what they are using or why. Your web browser is an important piece of computer software that allows you to visit web sites, and it is probably the most-used software on your computer.

Most noobies use whatever web browser came with their computer. For most PC owners running Windows, it's Internet Explorer (or the little blue 'e'), and for Mac owners it's Safari.

Understanding Your Web Browser

Web browsers communicate with web servers, turning pages and pages of programming code into a graphical representation that you can surf and enjoy. Because web browsers are free-standing software programs, you can download as many browsers as you want to your computer. When browsing, run them side by side to help you decide which one you like best or switch back and forth according to your needs. You may find that different browsers have different features you like for different tasks. And, some pages may look better on one browser over another.

Decoding Design Disasters

The variety of available web browsers and their frequent version updates poses a challenge for web designers. When creating a site, they must make sure each browser on each type of operating system (Mac OS X,

Windows, etc) is reading and interpreting the code correctly, giving you the visual representation they intended. More complicated designs and less thoroughly tested sites have a greater risk of miscommunication. So, if you come across a site where text and images are overlapping or menus aren't expanding the way they should, try opening the page in another browser for a better experience.

Making a Switch

Do you still feel indifferent about your browser? It plays an important role, and fortunately you have choices. Google has created a tool that helps you learn more about web browsers and encourages you to shop around. Going to http://www.whatbrowser.org, a tool created "by some folks at Google," will tell you what browser you currently are using. A one minute video does a great job of explaining the important role of your web browsing software, and you can follow links for downloading alternate browsers available for your computer.

Whether you stick with your current browser or you decide to make a switch, http://www.whatbrowser.org also provides instructions for customizing your currently running browser. These commonly requested tweaks will help tailor your browser experience. You can:

Change your homepage-decide what page you want to appear when you first launch your web browser.

Designate a search engine preference-this is the search engine that your browser will use when you type keywords into the browser's search field.

Choose a default browser-the default browser will open when you click on website links found in other applications like email or PDFs.

CHAPTER 19

MOSTLY USED PROGRAMMING LANGUAGES AND THEIR PROGRAMMING ADVANTAGES

Nowadays, world wide clients are demanding for cost effective solutions along with high-performance speedy development. In recent internet marketing arena, designing a good website template and placing unique and relevant content is not enough for a profitable web businesses. Web programming is getting more value in terms of building flexible websites. Web programmers are skilled in many programing platforms and satisfying the clients with their expertise.

In recent web industry as well as in software industry there are mainly three types of programming platforms getting famous in regards to their superb resource, their security and easy availability in the market and they are PHP platform, dot net platform and the java platform. These three programming platforms have their own advantages according to their work procedures

Advantages of Java programming

1. As a programming language Java is secure, multi-threaded, distributed, high-performance, object-oriented, robust, dynamic and portable in nature.

2. Java applets are platform independent and utilized for web programming.

3. Mobile applications made by Java is fully compatible with any mobile operating systems. In software development this is denoted as prime feature of Java mobile applications.

4. Enterprise Java Beans (EJB), Remote method Invocation (RMI) are globally accepted architecture for distributed systems.

5. Struts, CORBA, Hibernate, DAO are widely accepted Java architectures which fully support internationalization (i18n) for enterprise applications.

6. In Java programing, we can use any kind of database (paid or free) as per the client's requirement, i.e. for choosing database, Java programming language does not create any burden.

7. We all know that Java is a open source programming language and it is easily available in the market without any hassle.

Advantages of Dot Net programming

1. In Dot Net programing the programming codes and the HTML exist in different files.

2. Dot Net frame works are hugely used for doing specific applications.

3. Automatic garbage collection is possible in Dot Net programming.

4. Dot Net uses safe type cast and Strong and powerful IDE's for better and faster application development.

5. As this is a consistent programming model, it has got the direct support for security, in short Dot Net is highly secured programming language.

6. Dot Net provides an attribute called Serialization which is used for publishing or producing an item in the form of a series of information bits.

7. It is language independent, so if the team has multiple skill expertise like C#, Dot Net, C++, developers can still work on the same project with different skills set.

8. MS technologies provides RAD (rapid application development) to deliver project faster, because customers always prefer faster delivery.

9. Dot Net debugging is very effort-less therefore, can fix the bugs quicker.

Advantages of PHP programming

1. This programing language is accepted by maximum web programmers for its open source features.

2. PHP is a server side programing language that is widely used for web programming.

3. PHP language has some similarity with C and C++ programming. PHP syntax is quite similar to C and C++ syntax thus, a PHP programmer can easily learn it and make use of it in their respective works.

4. PHP programming language can run on both Windows and UNIX servers.

5. My-SQL is well known online database and can be interfaced very well with PHP. Therefore, PHP and My-SQL are an excellent combination for small business owners.

6. PHP language has got the powerful output buffering techniques that further increases over the output flow.

7. PHP can be used with a large number of relational database management systems, runs on all of the most popular web servers.

8. PHP5 is dynamic, platform independent and fully object oriented language that helps to build complex and large web applications.

CHAPTER 20

TIPS FOR AN EFFECTIVE AFFILIATE PROGRAM

1. What Is an Affiliate Management Program and Why Do You Need One?

Affiliate management programs allow you to effectively operate your affiliate program and the partnerships formed through it. You need effective affiliate management to ensure the highest ROI possible for all of your partnerships. Amazon.com is the poster child for a hugely successful affiliate management program. How did they do it? By using a robust affiliate management program and providing powerful tools and training to their affiliates.

2. Where Can You Find an Effective Affiliate Management Program?

Of course, Amazon's affiliate management program, code is proprietary, so you won't be able to get your hands on that, but you CAN get one. Then, just how can you get your own affiliate management program? It's simple, they're everywhere. If you type the phrase "affiliate management program" into your favorite search engine, you'll see a plethora of returned search results. Don't despair just yet; I'm going to tell you just what to look for in an effective affiliate management program.

But for now, you must decide if it's more of a benefit for you to buy and install an off-the-shelf software package on your server, or to pay for a hosted service, even if you have the expertise to easily install your own program. Does the boxed version do everything you need it to do? Is the price right? (Only you can decide that.)

3. Things to Look for In an Affiliate Management Program

Your affiliate management program should allow you to track your affiliates' progress, train them, contact them individually, and even make special arrangements with them (partnerships). A quality affiliate management program should immediately give you the information you need about your affiliates at a glance.

You should instantly be able to see who your best performing affiliates are and which ones are struggling. In this case, use the tools in your affiliate management program to email an automated training series to the affiliates who are having difficulty, or offer more personalized help. The choice is yours. On the flip-side of that, you can offer your best performers better incentives to keep the sales coming. Does your current affiliate management program allow you to do this?

4. What Are Multi-tiered Affiliate Management Programs

A multi-tiered affiliate management program is one that not only pays your affiliates commissions on the sales they make, but it also allows them to recruit others and make a percentage of their sales as well. Multi-tiered affiliate management programs are structured somewhat like MLM programs. They allow the top person to make a percentage of the sales of everyone else whom they recruit. Some affiliate programs go as deep as 5 levels, but these normally don't live up to expectations. It's like, "each one - teach one. The person directly above is responsible for the success of the person directly beneath them.

Two-tiered affiliate management programs usually work best for this. They are the most effective, as others don't pay as well on the 1st and 2nd levels (tiers) as the 2-tier affiliate management programs. Affiliate management programs that stretch beyond 2 levels may place the highest commission percentage to be earned on the lower levels - which are usually not filled. This prevents the affiliates from making the max commissions on their sales. It also provides little incentive for affiliates to keep promoting your product/service.

Therefore, for the best results I strongly recommend you use a two-tier affiliate management program if you're thinking of implementing a multi-tiered affiliate management program. Better yet, implement an affiliate management program that gives you the flexibility to offer a flat affiliate program, a 2-tiered affiliate program, or no program at all to your affiliates.

Look for an affiliate management program that's part of a package, or e-business suite. The package or suite should be a synergistic combination of e-business tools that you effectively manage and see the results of your efforts. For instance, you should be able to view your affilliates' stats, ads, and progress, etc. Don't make it harder that it has to be. Let the tools do the work for you by choosing the right tools upfront. So, you need a combination of powerful tools that automatically run and manage your affiliate program for you.

Offer your affiliates a chance to earn commissions, even recurring commissions through your affiliate management program. Let your affiliate program do the tracking

and expense calculations. You benefit by
instantly seeing which ads produce the best
results for you, and which ones you need to
toss. Then, everyone's happy - you and your
affiliates!

CHAPTER 20

A BRIEF HISTORY OF
ANTIVIRAL PROGRAMS

Just as computer viruses were first created
and recognized for their destructive potential
in the 1970s and 80s, antivirus programs
were then programmed to counter their
effects. Over time, viruses became more
sophisticated and better at eluding detection
and removal; some are so potent that they
can virtually take over your computer's
controls and eavesdrop on your computer
activities. They can disrupt your applications
and infect your PC or laptop by logging onto

your Internet Protocol (IP) address. Fortunately, antiviral programs also evolved to deal with these kinds of malware, and their features and capabilities were presented in more detail by both free antivirus reviews and computer magazines.

At the dawn of what is considered to be the Age of the Computer, viruses were not even given much thought then. The theory and concept behind them already existed and issues that are related to them popped up occasionally, but they are nothing in scope compared to their modern counterparts. The very first bona fide computer virus was actually programmed out of mischief and its creator never really took it seriously. So it is obvious that there is no requirement for any kind of software or application to deal with viruses.

However, during the middle part of the 1980s, things changed. The computer is now gaining public acceptance and they are now being introduced into homes and offices. As more computers are being used and networks are being established to connect them with each other, novice computer programmers put it upon themselves to create viruses that can compromise them. It amounted to a kind of sport to them to make viral programs and malware that can affect unsuspecting computer users and sabotage data; the more computers that their creation can infect, the more successful they will be seen. Thus the first antiviral program was released in 1987 to handle these viral threats.

At their inception there was very little need for antiviral software. They were first adopted by business owners and firms who see the need to secure important corporate data; home computer users, on the other hand, are not burdened with such concerns. Viruses during this time are only capable of deleting information from affected computer systems. If you backed up your hard drive frequently, this is enough to offset any viral actions. The Internet is still in its infancy and thus viruses are only propagated using floppy disks; the public don't have avenues to learn more about antiviral software such as free antivirus reviews. Antivirus protection would often take the form of the careful computer user knowing where to use their floppy disks and keeping them from getting infected.

However, when the Age of the Internet came about in the 1990s, viral programs suddenly have an easier and broader area of propagation, one that would give them virtually limitless access and anonymity. They are no longer dependent on storage media such as floppy disks to help them spread; all they have to do is to detect uninfected computers or take advantage of unsuspecting users and then wait for the right time to strike. During the Web's early years, a hacker can simply write a viral program that can con a computer user into accessing and then running it. Viruses during this time are mostly written via an executable program code. In response to them, the demand for antivirus applications now skyrocketed; paid and free antivirus reviews that analyzed them were also released.

The first antiviral programs were stock applications that can handle viruses and other malware using their own existing data. They are unable to keep up with new kinds of viruses because they were not updated, unlike those today that are constantly kept up-to-date. Antivirus software can only be revised on a monthly or even yearly basis. Nowadays, antiviral products generally go toe-to-toe with the latest viral threats. They are also geared to handle other types of malware such as spyware and adware. They also contain other utilities that can help protect your PC or laptop further such as firewalls and system checkers that can automatically scan your computer system and flag any viral actions that they come across.

Antiviral programs have a long history that follows that of computer viruses; they were there when viral infections were beginning to wreak havoc upon the computing public and will continue to exist so long as new and more complicated viruses and malware are being created with the potential of causing a computer virus pandemic. The danger is still there, but you will feel prepared to deal with them with the help of paid and free antivirus reviews that you can use to learn about the newest and latest antivirus applications, and then installing these antivirus programs in your computer.

CHAPTER 21

CRITERIA TO CHOOSE THE BEST ANTIVIRUS PROGRAM FOR YOUR NEEDS

There is no best antivirus program in general. You can make the best choice of your antivirus software depending of your goals, your needs and your environment. In order to choose your best antivirus software you should look at vendor information, independent antivirus certifying agencies reviews, as well as other sources. Here are the essential criteria for the right choice.

1. Compatibility

Antivirus program has to be compatible with your PC configuration. Your PC must meet hardware and software requirements of antivirus solution.

2. Range of Protection

Antivirus software should protect your PC from as many threats and on as many fronts as it can: viruses, worms, trojans, spyware, keyloggers, adware, rootkits, password stealers, phishing attacks, spam and others.

3. Effectiveness

Antivirus protection delivering by antivirus program should be effective and efficient. You may find and compare test results released by independent antivirus certifying agencies: Virus Bulletin, AV Comparatives, ISCA Labs, Westcoast Labs and others. If some antivirus solution was scored by these agencies high and consistently near the top, then you really can't go wrong with this top rated antivirus software.

4. Easy Installation

Good antivirus program has a prompt and easy installation. Interface should be clean, easy, and intuitive to use.

5. Easy to Use

Most users want to "install and forget" their antivirus software. So the best antivirus solution should have default configurations acceptable for most users. And at the same time good antivirus program can be easy configured and tweaked by advanced users.

6. Features

The best antivirus programs have the large features set that may include:

- list of compatible versions of Operational systems and platforms,

- amount of used system resources,

- using of proactive protection without false positives and with effective utilizing of system resources,

- availability of laptop battery saving mode,

- bootable rescue disk,

- silent gamer mode, and other available options.

A comprehensive features set adds strength to antivirus solution.

7. Update

The best security solutions have Automatic Update option and automatically perform updates every hour or "as needed updates" to keep virus definitions and program code up to date.

8. Support

The best security programs have comprehensive online and offline technical support. The program vendor should provide online knowledge base, FAQs, tutorials, user forums. The best vendors provide 24/7 support so you can ask your questions by phone, email or chat at any moment.

The best for your needs antivirus program delivers you the best security and usability with a minimal outlay of your time, money, or your PC system resources.

CHAPTER 22

COMPUTER PROGRAMMING BASICS - GETTING STARTED THE EASY WAY

A computer program is made up of a chain of instructions a computer has to perform. These instructions may come with other important data that's needed to carry out those instructions. Hence, the process of programming involves the defining of the instructions and the data. For you to come up with data for your computer, you should be familiar with computer programming basics and the datas three fundamental elements:

1. Instructions that need to be carried out.

2. Order in which the instructions are to be carried out.

3. Data needed to do the instructions.

The first stage of computer programming basically involves paper processes. In this phase, you don't even need to work using a computer, however if you use a word processor that will enable you to write your work to a disk file rather than in a piece of paper. You need to do this so you can figure out clearly and more specifically, what you want your computer to perform before you begin to instruct the computer to execute it.

Bear in mind that the computer will follow the instructions exactly as given. It can't say what you want; it can rather do what you want it to do. So before your program comes close to a computer, you need to do several steps which include:

- Defining the problem

Before you instruct the computer what to do, you must first be familiar with it. You need to clearly tell the computer what it needs to accomplish or to generate as the outcome of all the activities it will perform.

- Identifying the solution

If you already know what the computer will produce as an end result, you should take a close look at the information you have, and determine the information that you require. There's also a need for you to define the logical procedures, equations, and other methods you have to utilize so you can manipulate the raw input data into the end result you want to achieve.

- Mapping the solution

This stage in computer programming has to be laid out in proper order. Don't forget that the sequence in which actions are used is as vital as the actions themselves. When organizing the solution into the right order, you will be putting choices into consideration.

When you're done defining the problem as well as designing and mapping the solution, the next thing you need to do is to begin with the task of writing the program code into one or a couple of computer language(s). But before you proceed, you must first decide on the possible languages you need to use as well as the particular computer platform.

Usually, computer languages are optimized for various kinds of tasks. It is, hence, important to select first the language that will best suit the task required. Indeed, learning computer programming basics is the first step a wannabe programmer has to arm himself with, especially if he wants to pursue a career in the said field.

CHAPTER 23

TIPS ON EMBARKING ON A METATRADER PROGRAMMING PROJECT

MetaTrader programming converts trading ideas into useable software in a Forex platform. Although most providers and programmers have their own satisfaction guarantee policies, those policies are not enough for you to neglect proper communication procedures. In some cases wherein you are not satisfied with the program, you may get your money back, but not your wasted time and effort. Here are some tips to consider when embarkng on a MetaTrader software project:

Set clear goals. When describing the project, keep your statements clear and concise. Telling the provider that all you want is a profitable software would be absurd. Good programmers in MetaTrader know the terms used and the ins and outs of Forex trading, but there is no guarantee that they are also skilled financial analysts. In fact, most trading systems aren't profitable, and it would be up to the trader himself to optimize his trading strategy and mold its parameters to suit his needs.

Give keen and accurate details. Is the project for an indicator, script, or expert advisor? Are you going to use a third party software along with the finished program? Do you need trading data on the terminal for monitoring, or visual input on the screen for you to see? Relaying incomplete information can be costly, and you can end up always going back to the provider for technical support due to various errors and issues, and may even be charged more for program modifications.

State your desired parameters. Make it clear to the provider which of the factors on the software can be modified externally, such as money management, lot size and pip size multipliers, etc. This would allow you to modify your software without even looking at complex programming code. Also specify their default values so the programmer wouldn't set values you won't really use in live trading.

Determine the policies of your broker. Does your broker process order by market orders only? How many digits does your account trade in? These simple factors could save the trader a lot of time, especially during optimization, backtesting, and troubleshooting. It would always be helpful if you inform your provider regarding the broker you are going to use, so that they may use it on quality control before delivering the final program to you.

If possible, show examples and charts to illustrate your idea. Providing these information could help avoid a lot of communication gaps that would result to incorrect implementation for the program. This is especially helpful in cases wherein either the trader or the programmer is not a native English speaker.

Communication with providers is important when embarking on a MetaTrader programming project. Willingness to supply as much information as you can and attention to detail are necessary in order to ensure that the program would function according to your own trading strategy.

CHAPTER 24

PROBLEMS FACED BY NETWORK MARKETERS CAN BE SOLVED BY LEAD GENERATION PROGRAM

Lack of quality leads can be solved if you follow a genuine and workable lead generation program. Internet business suffers from this major form of trouble where very few people visit your website or purchase what you are willing to sell. So to fight this situation, you should generate or choosing an existing program that clicks.

If you are searching a program that is available on the market you have to look at some associated factors. Are the composers of the programs properly trained and have a successful background? Collect information of the developers and be sure of the genuineness before investing in their programs.

Lots of programs are advertised on the internet claiming about the secrets that can help you to bring in large number of clients. But the truth is that there is actually no such secret that can help you unless you have your own lead generation technique. Finding a lead generation program that will deliver highly qualified leads every day is not quite easy.

A correct program will add value to the business. Apart from increasing profits the programs should have value addition capacity that will help the prospective customers also. Through the program you will be able to attract customers and get new subscribers for your business. The leads generated everyday should be monetized properly. Unless you have a proper channel the leads will never increase.

The lead originator, the program coding and the contact directory - these three are very essential components of the program. Each of these must work in coordination without a glitch and if any part malfunctions the system can collapse. The essence is not only about creating the leads but also sustaining them. It is a continuing process that will go on till your business lasts. If the leads dry out business survival is impossible.

The program will only act as the business assistant. You have to play a major role by monitoring every sphere with care and maintain good relationship with your present customers as well as increase the members through good lead generation program.

CHAPTER 25

LEARN VIDEO GAME DESIGN AND PROGRAMMING BY ATTENDING A SUMMER CAMP

The industry of video game design is an extraordinarily creative industry and very similar to the Hollywood movie making industry. A diverse group of people with a lot of different skills work together as a team to create a movie, and the same thing happens in the creation of a video game.

The Industry needs, and actively looks for people that are highly creative, great team players, and highly skilled in a variety of disciplines. This is a fact of life in the world of making games and it is a dramatic change from industries that have been around a long time. This is not our father's work world. It is exactly these three components that a summer camp offers a teen. It gives the attendees a creative environment where teamwork is developed and specific computer skills are learned.

If you are considering going to a camp for designing games there are a couple of things you should think about. First of all, the world of game making is very diverse and there are a lot of different programs and applications that can be used, so you have to consider what areas of game making you are interested and then look for a camp that covers that. A good example of what I mean is that you can learn how to design levels, program code, make java games, create 3d models, or any number of other things. There are also quite a few different programs that you could master from 3ds MAX for modeling to FPS Creator for level and game design. And what you want to do in the realm of game making will determine which skills and applications you should learn.

So, you should carefully consider what kinds of things about making video games appeal to you and try to find a camp that will fill that requirement. If you are a parent considering sending a teen or child to a camp you should spend time talking with him or her about what is interesting about video games. Chances are good he or she will know more about making games than you do. Your teen may like three-dimensional modeling, graphic design, writing or level design. This is a big factor in whether the camp will be a success or not. It's a matter of fulfilling individual goals and needs.

Your first course of action in looking for a summer camp should be to check with your local University or Community College. Just about every institution like this has summer learning programs for kids and teens. And unless you are already a student there you probably would never learn about the programs being offered so all it takes is a phone call and a request for a brochure. If geographic location is not a big concern for

213

you there are plenty of top grade institutions that offer one week or two week long programs.

Summer camps are a great way to immerse a teen or child in the highly creative world of video game design and programming. It is a great way to get a feel for the career potential in the industry. And as a bonus he or she is actually going to come home from the camp with a real and complete video game that he or she made!

CHAPTER 26

SOLVE YOUR PROGRAMMING QUERIES WITH CUSTOM SOFTWARE DEVELOPMENT COMPANY

With the global technological development, internet has helped the entire world to stay webbed. Online presence of a company is an effective tool for staging trade towards growth and profit. In order to get cost effective and quality ways for developing websites, it is always beneficial to go with the offshore IT development companies. These days numerous trading companies are expanding their business ends with the help of software development companies in IT sector.

Offshore companies have a lot to offer you from a small software application to an entire web product. You can achieve competent web solutions for your different types of trading ends. There are few principles that one must follow while opting for a perfect offshore IT development company. The cost of the software development is a great matter that suggests the cost of the entire project. It is wise for not negotiate over the quality of the web development for lower cost. To avoiding the bad quality services one can go with offshore companies offering customized services in IT.

Go with a custom software development company that considers the bespoke requirement of its clients. Checking over the experience and team strength is the best way to find out the appropriate development company for your project. Always check with the exact hands-on experience of the software company and their team efficiency to ensure the quality of you project. The development company must be working over the updated technologies to meet unambiguous business requirements. A software company should work according to the global standards to provide great software solutions. It is good to have a look over the previous work of the company to determine the quality of the work they deliver.

There are various software companies offering global solutions through custom

ASP.NET application development in India. For customized software solutions, one can refer to the efficient offshore dot net software development companies. All these companies are capable of fulfilling your programming ends in a personalized manner. ASP.Net is an object-oriented web development procedure where developers use a library to encrypt the programming codes.

To get high-end solutions for your development project it is important to consider the unique quality of your programming. With custom ASP.NET application development, you will be able to reach global clients by setting your unique work style. One can even hire developers on hourly basis, daily basis and monthly basis suiting your requirements. With so many options revealed it is easy to select for result-oriented programming.

SOFTWARE TESTING: USING A TRACKING TOOL INCREASES PROGRAM DEPENDABILITY

Software development entails various steps for ensuring the final product functions appropriately and is bug free. Testing occurs throughout the programming life cycle to verify individual feature quality as well as the overall performance of the application. It may be performed during the creation of a consumer product or prior to implementing a new system within an organization. In commercial environments, software testing assists with the identification of defects that will prevent a consumer from completing necessary tasks. Business testing involves verifying if required processes will work correctly to prevent additional system downtime. Application creation includes a revolving cycle where requirements are defined, designed as features, coded by the development team, tested for defects, sent back to the programmer for corrections, and then evaluated again before a system is put into place or the product is released. The cycle can occur countless times before the final product is deemed as ready for use. Programmers require reliable tools to manage the numerous tasks put on them when working on varying sized projects. One missed issue can affect the entire functionality of a system or program. Tracking tools offer a simple method for managing the responsibilities of developers, testers, and engineers.

Task Tracking Software: A Vital Tool to Application or System Development

Testing makes sure requirements have been met, verifies appropriate functionality, and helps an organization determine if characteristics will remain intact upon installation. The process takes place at varying times throughout the development process including at the end of large milestones and when a specific feature requires further evaluation. In most programming scenarios, the bulk of testing occurs after requirement defining and coding are completed. It is during this time when engineers or support professionals go through each feature many times in an effort to find defects or missing functionality. Any found item is brought to the attention of management who then assigns the issue to an individual or team of developers for correction. Task tracking software may be utilized to define initial design responsibilities, keep track of coding requirements, or to manage problem resolution throughout the development cycle.

Application testing may be static or dynamic in nature depending on the evaluation goals a company is attempting to achieve. Static testing involves performing a walk through of the system or having a customer review the beta version. Dynamic processes entail the usage of test cases to verify programmed code is functioning as desired. The overall goal of various testing procedures is to verify the software or system has been built correctly and meets specific consumer needs. Task tracking software aids in the process by providing a central information source where all development parties can enter, monitor, and organize responsibilities regarding one or more projects. These applications may be integrated with other organizational tools to create a solid project management solution. Tracking tools are not limited to development environments and may be utilized by multiple organizational departments to obtain improved productivity in daily activities or non-software related projects. Software testing is only one example of where an application can improve product quality and organization throughout a company.

CODE IGNITER WEB DEVELOPMENT: A POPULAR PHP FRAMEWORK

Here is yet another treat for all those developers who use PHP as their main platform to design and develop engaging and dynamic websites. Yes, we are talking about Code Igniter web development. We know that there are a whole lot of significant open source frameworks in Codeigniter Web Development are put to use for getting rapid web application development. Code Igniter web development framework remains the most popular one in the category. This too comes in the MVC pattern which facilitates the web developers in transforming the illustrative as well as innovative concepts that the users come up with into real applications. For people who shun away any kind of complexity and would want effective and simple solutions, it is then Code Igniter for them definitely.

The main benefit that one can get with the help of Code Igniter is competent solutions in web development that render effective service to the users. It is beneficial not only for the users but for the developers too. As there are a rich set of libraries, the developers can accomplish a wide range of web applications and development services faster. Providing an easy interface coupled with logical structure to gain access to the libraries is the main feature that Code Igniter bestows its users.

With the help of Code Igniter one can get websites that are fully functional and they come about in absolutely simple structure. Managing the web applications also becomes absolutely easy without much ado about anything and the websites offer steadfast performance too. This is one highly secure development platform that the developers can make use for a wide range of applications. The development process is absolutely transparent as there is thorough and clear documentation. One can get a whole lot of flexible applications with the help of customized features that are a part of Code Igniter framework.

This is search engine friendly and hence when it comes in with clean URLs there is definitely a prominent online presence for the website. It is strongly believed that Code

Igniter offers a very fast and reliable platform for development. A simple interface yet robust range of libraries enables faster development of the web projects in comparison to the writing of programming codes is what makes this framework a special one.

The Code Igniter framework is the most preferred framework by huge business conglomerates as it is an effective and light weight platform to create applications which have to deal with huge amounts of data as well as security purposes for the applications that come out of this platform are considered to be highly secure and absolutely dependable.

Yet another main reason why big enterprises opt for this framework is that they do not have to spend a whole lot of time in coding and structuring the coding. TechiesTown InfoTech claims to offer customized Code Igniter framework services across expansive industry verticals throughout the globe. Development, deployment, complete implementation, maintenance and support are the services that the company claims to offer its clients. If you are looking out for a simple yet reliable web development solution, then perhaps Code Igniter is the one for you!

CHAPTER 27

<u>LOAD PERFORMANCE TESTING - BE SURE THAT YOUR SOFTWARE PROGRAM OPERATES COMPLETELY</u>

Building programs and also sites may be fun and then difficult all at once, however when complete, you'll have a sense of fantastic achievement for your own efforts, but imagine if the end package just didn't match customer or client requirements - and much more significantly, what if the product failed at the time of use?

The task of a typical developer (whether creating for the web, local computer solutions or some other areas), is loaded with long hours of clearing up computer code, increasing the user experience and ensuring that just about all features of this project work seamlessly. They're going to also need to find flaws on their own in their programming, and offer improvements to keep the software program continually accessible. How can these people accelerate the process?

Working With Software Programs For Stress Tolerance:

Before even setting up the project, you need to have a certain comprehension of what individuals might be making use of it, the total number of customers may very well be hooked up at any one single time, as well as how they'll use this too. Building a program only really suitable for a small number of connections, which can be subsequently flooded with a large number of end users will inevitably result in a system failure, probably doing harm to your project and your reputation.

This is why it is recommended to perform stress assessments. Load and performance tests are the process where you actually push your website or maybe software program to the limits, and analyse the results retrieved to determine if there are actually any faults, the way the program responded and also whether you'll be able to or even need to make changes. The main advantages to this will be:

- You could quickly and easily diagnose whether your project is able to deal with a high amount of users at a single time

- Make sure your project doesn't dissatisfy people as a result of program overload

- Improve speed and overall performance of your respective task through identifying essential areas and processes which respond slowly.

How Will You Perform Load Testing?

If you don't have access to 1000s of computer systems (and also have enough individuals to start using these at the same time!), you are going to of course need to look for any better strategy to stress test your programs, the most affordable and useful technique is by using load testing software.

These programs are usually marketed as performance testing software, and have been developed for this single function. They will enable you to alter lots of variables to ensure a precise evaluation of your respective project, replicating genuine human behavior, and also letting you specify the quantity of connections are to be used throughout every testing phase.

It's a wise course of action to run several tests, raising the quantity of end users for every session to actually obtain a clear picture of your respective software programs greatest operating levels. If you discover your site or perhaps programs are going to be connected to by a larger amount of persons - you'll know this could be leading to slow downs in calculating data, or maybe total failures for quite a few customers, and you might require to recreate your program code or improve upon it.

If you think maybe that performance and load testing is outside your very own capabilities, you could hire a third party company to get this done for you.

MICROSOFT ACCESS VALIDATION OF DATA USING ONE LINE OF CODE

Microsoft Access validation of data using one line of code is possible using the code in this two part article. Data validation checks that data are valid, sensible, and reasonable before they are processed. Microsoft Access validation can involve a time consuming choir if one had to do it for each control or 'access field', on each of your Access forms. Several have authored various approaches to automate Access validation for you. No single approach will work for all situations. Your form might allow a user to move off the record before Microsoft Access validation code is triggered. If you try to prevent the user from doing so, you will need to create additional design changes and add more complexity to your form. Here is a conservative approach to Access validation, which works for most situations.

The user is notified if a form control failed validation, told why it failed, the control is highlighted briefly, and cursor focus is moved back to the failing control. Oh yes, it doesn't try to validate form controls that come later, in the tab order, than where the

231

user currently is. A single line of programming code is used on the OnOpen event of your form for this Microsoft Access validation of form data. The user can be prevented from navigating off the form record, adding a new record, or closing the form if validation fails, this requires an additional line of code on the appropriate form close, add new record and navigation buttons.

So how does it work? An Access developer just needs to enter a few characters into the 'TAG' property of a form's control. The 'TAG' control property stores extra information about a control.

A subroutine called 'SetValidatorEventHandlers' is place in the OnOpen Event of every form you want Microsoft Access validation of form data. It will add the call to the Validator function from OnGotFocus Events of all visible text box, combo boxes, and listboxes on your form. If you already are planning to place other code in the OnGotFocus Events of these controls on your form, then you will want to reference the custom validation function call 'Validator' in the OnGotFocus subroutine for each control that you will want to trigger this code.

Place in the 'Tag' property of each control you want to validate the following symbols and characters:

* *n - The form control may not be left empty.

* *d - The control must contain a valid date.

* *+ - The control must have an amount greater than zero.

* *@ -The control must be a valid email address.

Other types of validation may be added by you as needed. You may may combine these pairs of characters if needed.

If you do not wish to refer to the form's controls actual name in your validation message to the user, you may specify a preferred alternative name by adding this to the end of the tag property.

~My Preferred Control Name

Replace 'My Preferred Control Name' with the control name you want the user to see.

CONCLUSION

The average computer is packed with hidden software that can secretly spy on online habits.

The US net provider EarthLink said it uncovered an average of 28 spyware programs on each PC scanned during the first three months of the year.

There are currently over 38,000 spyware and adware programs that are infecting innocent Internet users such as yourself through downloadable games, music, screensavers, pictures, pop-ups, emails, and the list goes on and on. Spyware and Adware can cause your PC to run extremely slow and even crash, and allow hackers and advertising companies to invade your privacy whenever they wish.

What Is Spyware?

Spyware is a broad term for programs that collects information from your computer without your knowledge or consent.

Spyware is a software program that transmits a unique code to identify you (for tracking purposes) without your knowledge or consent. The programs collects or transmits information about your computer use, or other habits without your knowledge or consent.

This internet pest which is better known as spyware installs itself on your computer without your knowledge or consent. It performs other unwholesome duties, and continue to reinstalling itself no matter how many times you remove it.

Spyware!

It has become so pervasive that lawmakers in the US are looking into ways to prevent or regulate it. The Spy Audit by EarthLink reflects the results of scans involving over one million computers between January and March. It uncovered more than 29.5 million examples of spyware.

Why should I be concerned about spyware or adware?

Passwords, credit card details and other personal information could end up in the wrong hands.

Your computer could get unwanted viruses, worms or even Trojan.

You would receive unwanted emails.

Your computer could be used by malicious operators to do damage not only your own computer, but to other computer users too.

How did I get spyware on my computer and how do I eliminate it?

It usually happens when you visit a web site, and are prompted to download something that is said to be "necessary" to view or use features of that web site. Also, you might want or download a program that has some nice features, but also installs program code that can send information out without your knowledge.

"By tracking and publicizing the growth of spyware, we can better educate consumers of its risks and encourage them to take steps to protect themselves and their families while online," said Christine Stevenson of Webroot, which conducted the scans.

People concerned about what might be lurking on their machine can download software such as the popular ZoneAlarm Pro to disinfect their computer.

REFERENCES

[1] Lieberman, H., 2007. End-User Software Engineering Position Paper. In: End-User Software Engineering Dagstuhl Seminar.

[2] Burnett M M, Engels G, Myers B A, Rothermel G, 2007, End-User Software Engineering Dagstuhl Seminar, http://eusesconsortium.org/docs/dagstuhl_20 07.pdf.

[3] De Souza, C., 2007. Designers Need End-User Software Engineering. In: End-User Software Engineering Dagstuhl Seminar.

[4] Ko, A. J., 2007. Barriers to Successful End-User Programming. In: End-User Software Engineering Dagstuhl Seminar.

[5]   Drag   and   Drop,   2007,
http://www.cems.uwe.ac.uk/amrc/seeds/Aja
x/components.html.

[6]   Scand   dhtmlxTree,   2007,
[http://www.scbr.com/docs/products/dhtmlx
Tree/index.shtml].

[7] Repenning, A., 2007. End-User Design.
In: End-User Software Engineering
Dagstuhl Seminar.

[8] Rosson, M. B., A., 2007. Position paper
for EUSE 2007 at Dagstuhl. In: End-User
Software Engineering Dagstuhl Seminar.

[9] Coutaz, J., 2007. Meta-User Interfaces
for Ambient Spaces: Can Model-Driven-
Engineering Help?. In: End-User Software
Engineering Dagstuhl Seminar.

[10] Programming with XML, 2007, http://www.cems.uwe.ac.uk/amrc/seeds/PeterHale/XML/XML.htm#ProgrammingwithXML.

Do not go yet; One last thing to do

If you enjoyed this book or found it useful I'd be very grateful if you'd post a short review on it. Your support really does make a difference and I read all the reviews personally so I can get your feedback and make this book even better.

Thanks again for your support!